They Broke The Law – You Be The Judge

True Cases Of Teen Crime

Judge Tom Jacobs
Edited By Al Desetta

16pt

Copyright Page from the Original Book

Copyright © 2003 by Thomas A. Jacobs, J.D.

All rights reserved under International and Pan-American Copyright Conventions. Unless otherwise noted, no part of this book may be reproduced, stored in a retrieval system, or transmitted in any form or by any means, electronic, mechanical, photocopying, recording or otherwise, without express written permission of the publisher, except for brief quotations or critical reviews. For more information, go to www.freespirit.com/company/permissions.cfm.

Free Spirit, Free Spirit Publishing, and associated logos are trademarks and/or registered trademarks of Free Spirit Publishing Inc. A complete listing of our logos and trademarks is available at www.freespirit.com.

Library of Congress Cataloging-in-Publication Data
Jacobs, Thomas A.
    They broke the law, you be the judge : true cases of teen crime / Thomas A. Jacobs.
       p. cm.
Summary: Letters from and interviews with twenty-one children and teenagers who broke the law reveal what it is like to be arrested, attend legal proceedings, and be held accountable for one's actions.
Includes bibliographical references and index.

1. Juvenile justice, Administration of—United States—Juvenile literature. 2. Juvenile delinquents—United States—Juvenile literature. [1. Justice, Administration of 2. Juvenile delinquents. 3. Crime. 4. Juvenile courts.] I. Title.
    KF9780.J33 2003
    345.73'08—dc21

2003004814

Free Spirit Publishing does not have control over, or assume responsibility for, author or third-party websites and their content. At the time of this book's publication, all facts and figures cited within are the most current available. All telephone numbers, addresses, and website URLs are accurate and active; all publications, organizations, websites, and other resources exist as described in this book; and all have been verified as of May 2010. If you find an error or believe that a resource listed here is not as described, please contact Free Spirit Publishing. Parents, teachers, and other adults: We strongly urge you to monitor children's use of the Internet.

Reading Level Grades 7 & Up; Interest Level Ages 12 & Up;
Fountas & Pinnell Guided Reading Level Z

Cover and interior design by Marieka Heinlen

15 14 13 12 11 10 9 8
Printed in the United States of America
V20280710

Free Spirit Publishing Inc.
217 Fifth Avenue North, Suite 200
Minneapolis, MN 55401-1299
(612) 338-2068
help4kids@freespirit.com
www.freespirit.com

TABLE OF CONTENTS

Introduction	iv
A Brief Look at the Juvenile Justice System	xi
How to Use This Book	xvii
Using Role Plays	xxvi
Glossary of Legal and Court Terms Used in the Book	xxx
ADAM, 15	1
ADELINA, 13	19
ANDREW, 17	40
ASHLEY, 14	58
BRANDON, 14	76
BRIANNE, 17	94
CARLA, 15	115
CHARLES, 16	134
ERICA, 14	152
JENNIFER, 13	169
JERRY, 15	188
JOSHUA, 15	204
MARCUS, 14	220
NATALIE, 14	234
OLIVIA, 14	249
PHILIP, 9	269
RONALD*, 16	287
SAMANTHA, 14	301
SEAN, 16	319
STARLETT, 14	335
TANYA, 14	354
Closing Arguments	373
Resources	375
About the Author	393

Other Great Books from Free Spirit	395
Index	399

Praise for *They Broke the Law—You Be the Judge*

"A refreshing and completely unique resource."
—*Youthworker*

"Teachers and students looking for a great primer on criminal law should look no further than this book."
—*KLIATT*

"Unusual and thought-provoking.... With the proliferation of courtroom shows on television, this book gives young people a more realistic look at the legal system designed for them."
—*School Library Journal*

"Through the encouraged role-playing, students will gain a better understanding of the intricacies of the system. An excellent introduction of how juvenile justice works, this will be a great resource for classroom and group discussions."
—*Booklist*

Dedication

This book is dedicated to Jacque Steiner, who has spent decades working with and for children and teens. Her devotion to our youth is unparalleled in its sincerity and scope. My wife Gail and I have been blessed and inspired to know Jacque and her husband, Fred.

Acknowledgments

This book would have never been written were it not for the support and assistance of a few good friends. In addition to the brave individuals profiled here, and their parents and family members, I extend heartfelt appreciation to Dave Lawrence, Kylie Knape, Erica Melissa, Sheila Sailer, Judge Linda Scott, Jacque Steiner, Susan Tone, Cherie Townsend, and Jon Davis Wiley.

Thanks also to Judy Galbraith and Free Spirit Publishing, for the opportunity to talk to America's youth. My editor, Al Desetta, did a masterful job of reworking the original manuscript. His guidance and encouragement throughout this project are truly appreciated. Thanks, Al. And a word of appreciation goes to Darsi Dreyer for her editing assistance and to Marieka Heinlen for her design work in the book and the awesome cover. Thanks to both.

Introduction

This book contains true stories about teens and crime. You'll read about 21 young people who broke the law and came before my court for sentencing. The facts are exactly as they happened and nothing has been changed. As a juvenile court judge, I had to hold them responsible for their crimes and decide on the right punishment.

THEY BROKE THE LAW

Most of these teens were nervous when they came to court. Some were scared. None of them wanted to be there. But almost all were sorry for what they did and were willing to accept responsibility.

Some of their crimes were relatively minor. Joshua, 15, was arrested for cutting school. Natalie, 14, was caught with beer at a party. Other offenses were more serious. Adam, 15, threatened to kill kids at his school. Charles, 16, was caught with cocaine and a gun. Brianne, 17, committed car theft, credit card theft, and forgery.

These cases raised difficult issues for me as a judge. Sean, 16, had a pipe bomb in his bedroom, but claimed he was only going to set it off in a field, not near people or property. Could I believe him? Philip, 9, was arrested for spitting in his mother's face. How should I, as a judge, deal with someone that young? Should Philip even be in court? Tanya, 14, was arrested for shoplifting a pregnancy test kit. What was more important—to punish Tanya for stealing or to help a young girl who might be pregnant?

As a judge, I had to decide how to be fair in each case. Samantha, 14, took a cab when she ran away from an abusive home and was arrested for not paying the fare. Olivia, also 14, stole a car. Both girls came before my court, but they had committed very different crimes. Their needs were different and the court's response had to fit their individual cases. What could the juvenile justice system do for them so they wouldn't show up in my court again?

YOU BE THE JUDGE

This book puts you in the role of answering these and other hard questions. You'll see these cases unfold, as they did before me. You'll be asked to step into my shoes—to become a juvenile court judge and determine how a teenager should be held responsible for her crime.

Many of the teens in this book have faced similar family problems, such as divorce, living with one parent, poverty, drug abuse, or domestic violence. Family problems are never an excuse for crime, but you will be asked to take into consideration the young person's background in determining the appropriate punishment and services. You will have all of the information that was available to me at the time of sentencing.

For each case, you're given a list of sentencing options, which include jail and probation, but also programs and resources like family counseling, drug treatment, and anger management classes. You have to find a balance between protecting your community from the juvenile and rehabilitating the juvenile—helping him to turn his life around. Don't limit yourself to the sentencing options outlined in each profile. If you have an idea for an appropriate penalty or service that is not listed, write it down and discuss it with others. Think not only in terms of the person who committed the crime, but of the family as a whole. You can also think of how to help the victim.

After passing sentence on the young person, discuss what you did and listen to what your friends or classmates decided. What have you learned about the juvenile justice system from choosing a sentence? Was there anything about the young person's family life or background that influenced your decision? Do you have a better understanding of teens and crime? Are there changes you would like to see in how the system works?

You will find out the actual sentence these young people got and what happened to them afterwards. Many of them—like most teens—committed one crime and never got into trouble again. Others were repeat offenders who promised me in court and in letters that they would change their behavior, only to end up back in front of me a few weeks or months later. Several are currently in jail or on the run. But most have their problems under control and are working, going to school, and leading normal lives. These are courageous kids who, despite the odds, have managed to survive.

Juvenile court hearings are serious business, and the majority of young people I've seen take the situation seriously. I've had teens in my court apologize to their victims. Others have written letters to me. One of them sparked the idea for this book.

It was a letter by Marcus, who was 14 when he was arrested for shoplifting. He wrote the following to the owner of the store:

> **Dear Sir/Madam,**
> **My name is Marcus. I tried to steal a telephone cord from your store. I don't know why I did it, because I know it is wrong to steal. My mother has always taught me that if I want**

> *something bad enough, I can earn the money to buy it. I hate the pain I see in my mother's eyes because I know that I caused it. I hate the guilt that I feel, but I caused that too. I hate the example that I set for my little sister because I am supposed to be a role model for her. I am very ashamed of myself, and I promise you that I will never try to steal anything ever again.*
>   *Sincerely,*
>   *Marcus*

I've heard similar expressions quite often in my courtroom. It is said that you learn more from listening than speaking. After 30 years as a lawyer and judge, most of which was spent in juvenile court, I can tell you it's true. I've learned a wealth of information from listening to parents, victims, witnesses, and, most importantly, to the teenagers who came to my court for trial and sentencing.

By putting you in my shoes, I hope this book will help you learn as much

as I did and perhaps answer some of your questions about how our juvenile justice system works. And I think you will be as touched by these young people's stories as I was.
    Tom Jacobs

A Brief Look at the Juvenile Justice System

Through the 1800s, children and teenagers in the United States were considered the property of their parents and, no matter how young, weren't given special treatment if they got into trouble with the law. They were tried and, if found guilty, were sent to jail or institutionalized. Troublemakers were sent to "reform school," where kids were disciplined by putting them in isolation and not feeding them. The first priority was punishment and what was best for the community, not what would help the young people turn their lives around.

Then, in 1899, the efforts of reformers to save delinquent teenagers resulted in the creation of the first juvenile court system. The philosophy of this new court was rehabilitation—its purpose was not to punish, but to help the juvenile mend his or her ways. The question shifted from whether the juvenile committed the crime, to the best thing that the court could do for him or her.

Still, during most of the 1900s, there was no set of laws in this country that protected teenagers' rights. State laws varied, and kids could be treated differently depending on where they lived. For example, in some areas curfew violations and truancy were punished, while in other parts of the country such violations were either ignored or no law existed at all. It was almost 70 years before the United States Supreme Court decided a case involving the rights of juveniles. It took that long before kids were recognized as persons with individual rights under the law.

In the famous Gault case (387 U.S. 1, 1967), the Supreme Court reviewed the case of 15-year-old Gerry Gault, who had been arrested for making an offensive telephone call to a neighbor. Gerry told the police that he only dialed the number and his friend took the phone and made the comments. At the time of this incident, Gerry, like most teenagers, had no rights. Neither he nor his parents were told of the charge against him in writing, nor were they given written notice of his hearing. Gerry was not told he could have a lawyer, that he could call witnesses on his behalf, and that he could question the victim. In fact, the victim didn't even appear at Gerry's hearing. Gerry was found guilty because of the statements of a probation officer and was sent off to a state school, where he was basically locked up for two years.

In reviewing Gerry's case, the Supreme Court ruled that the Bill of Rights is not only for adults—its protections apply to juveniles as well. The rights given adults in criminal cases should also be available to Gerry and all teenagers.

As a result of Gault, teenagers are now entitled to receive notice of any criminal charge filed against them and have the right to have an attorney represent them. They also have the right to remain silent and the protection of the Fifth Amendment to not incriminate (testify against) themselves. In other words, the juvenile does not have to talk about the incident with the police or anyone else. The prosecutor has to prove the charge without the juvenile's help. There are additional rights the juvenile may have depending on the laws of each state (such as posting bail, a jury trial, etc.).

Since Gerry's case, teen rights have been expanded to include situations involving freedom of expression, religion, and speech, as well as protection against unreasonable searches and seizures. For example, kids can wear buttons or T-shirts with messages to school, as long as they're not disruptive to the school environment; kids can start a Bible club or a gay-lesbian club in school if other clubs are allowed; teens have a reasonable expectation that their pockets, backpacks, and purses won't be searched, depending on the circumstances. These rights, however, are balanced with the authority parents and others (like schools) have over their children.

Each state sets its own age limit for juvenile cases—either 18, 19, 20, or 21. This is important because the penalties in adult court can be more severe than those in juvenile court. For example, a teen sentenced in juvenile court may be locked up for a crime, but only for a limited time (up to age 18, 19, 20, or 21). An adult, however, may be sentenced to spend many years in prison or on probation.

If a young person is found guilty in juvenile court, a sentencing (or disposition) takes place. The judge considers the facts of the case, the juvenile's history, and all relevant information about the family and victim. The judge then decides the penalty, which may include jail, probation, community service, a fine, educational classes, counseling, or payment to the victim.

The judge is not limited to these options and may include an additional penalty or service, depending on the needs of the juvenile. Creative, individualized sentencing works with many teens. The goal is to balance punishment with helping the young person.

Of the 30 million teenagers in the United States, less than 5 percent have contact with juvenile court. Even fewer end up in jail. Most teens charged with a crime receive a penalty from the court and don't come back. The message received from the judge is loud and clear, resulting in a small number of repeat offenders.

The juvenile justice system affects all of us, one way or another. You may be the relative or friend of a teen who has committed a crime or who has been the victim of a crime. You may want to see changes and reforms in the juvenile justice system. Or you may want to pursue a career as a lawyer, judge, social worker, parole officer, police officer, or corrections officer. A knowledge of how the system works is the first step in becoming involved.

How to Use This Book

This book contains 21 true stories of teens and crime. Each story is organized the same way.

THE TEEN'S BACKGROUND LEADING UP TO THE CRIME

Here we describe the teen's background before he committed the crime—his family life, attitudes toward school, and previous run-ins with the law. You get a glimpse of the home situation. Are the parents together? Divorced? Is the family struggling to make ends meet? Have other family members gotten in trouble with the law? Much of this information will help you decide what sentence and services the young person should receive.

THE CRIME THAT WAS COMMITTED

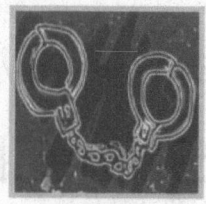

The young person's crime is described: how it was committed, against whom, how the police were notified, and the young person's reaction to getting caught.

Occasionally we'll explain legal or court terms in a box, so you understand how the juvenile justice system works.

Legal Definitions of the Crime Committed

Here we give the legal definition of the crime committed by the young person.

YOUR CONCERNS AS A JUDGE

In this part of the profile, you're given more background on the young person since her arrest. Does she have a drug problem? Is she a repeat offender? Does she have a history of running away from home? What are your worries or concerns about this young person? How can you find a balance between holding her responsible for her crime and helping her?

YOUR SENTENCING OPTIONS AS A JUDGE

The sentencing options are explained here. You are asked to choose from a range of punishments and services: jail time, probation, community service, fines or payments to the victim, individual and family counseling, placement in foster care, placement in a drug treatment program, writing a letter to the victim or the judge, and several others. You can choose one option or several in combination.

You also have the freedom to come up with your own ideas for sentencing, as juvenile court judges do in real courtrooms. For example, if someone is caught with alcohol in a car, you might have that young person do community service in a hospital emergency room, where he can see what happens to people who drive drunk. Or if someone shoplifted from a store, you may order that youth to write a letter of apology to the store owner. Or you may want to order all family members to participate in counseling together.

Feel free to come up with your own ideas for sentencing.

QUESTIONS TO CONSIDER BEFORE SENTENCING

We ask you a series of questions to get you to think more closely about the pros and cons of the various sentencing options. Should a 14-year-old go to jail for making a threat in school? Will the young person be harmed or hurt by jail? A 16-year-old doesn't want to go to anger management classes, even though she has a big problem with her temper. Should you order her to go anyway? You suspect that one girl, age 14, might be abused at home, but you have no evidence. Do you remove her from the home and place her in foster care until you investigate the family more? Or should she be given a second chance at home. Another young girl, 17, has run away or been kicked out from every program the court has placed her in and the threat of jail doesn't scare her. What do you do with her?

These are hard questions to answer, but these are the same questions a juvenile court judge has to answer every day.

YOU BE THE JUDGE

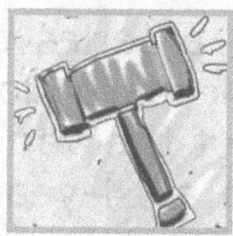

Based on the information you have, we ask you to pass sentence on the young person. You can write it down or discuss it with others.

WHAT ACTUALLY HAPPENED

Here you find out the sentence the young person actually got in real life, his reaction to it, and the judge's explanation of why he gave that sentence.

YOUR RESPONSE TO THE JUDGE'S DECISION

You have a chance to respond to the judge's decision. How is it different from yours? Is it harder or easier on the young person? Do you agree or disagree with the actual sentence the teen got? Why? You can write down or discuss your reaction.

Letter from the Young Person

The profiles include letters by the young person to the judge. Some letters were written before the young person was sentenced, some were written from jail, and others were written after the young person had gotten her life together. All the letters are in the young person's own words. You'll get a sense of who they are and

> *how they feel about what happened to them.*

THE YOUNG PERSON TODAY

We give you an update about what the young person is doing today. Some kids are in jail or on the run, but most are going to school or working and trying to make something of themselves.

FINAL THOUGHTS

Here you have a chance to sum up your feelings about the story you read. Do you think the young person was treated fairly by the system? Could anything have been done differently?

Are you surprised about how the young person's life turned out? Has the young person's story made you think differently about issues you face at home, in school, or in your community? Do you look at your peers in a different way? At the juvenile justice system in a different way? You can write down or discuss your thoughts.

Did You Know?

Many of the profiles end with a few statistics or information related to the young person's case.

Using Role Plays

When readers are asked to pass sentence, they can write down or discuss their thoughts. Another option is to conduct a role play of the sentencing hearing. One young person can play the judge, another can play the juvenile. Parents, family members, and victims can also be played as roles.

Acting out these parts can help teens connect emotionally with the issues, conflicts, and challenges faced by the judge and the teens. Role plays can also teach the importance of listening carefully and working cooperatively. No special training is needed, just a clear understanding of some basic guidelines:
- Explain the purpose of the role play to the group—to help them better understand the issues raised by each story. Mention that the volunteers will not be playing themselves, but will portray what the judge or young person would say at sentencing.

- Explain that the facilitator might ask for action to be frozen, or that the audience or facilitator might provide instruction or feedback while the role play is going on.
- Role plays can be done simultaneously in dyads or triads (groups of two or three young people). This can warm up the group to role plays with minimal embarrassment. When finished, the smaller groups can discuss their role plays. Then ask volunteers to repeat the role play in front of the larger group.
- Review the story before beginning the role play.
- Ask teens to volunteer to play the judge and the young person. (For some stories, you can ask for volunteers to play family members or victims.) If no one volunteers, one solution is to offer to play one part yourself. This will usually get one teen to join you.
- Once you've picked two (or more) volunteers, quickly review what they might say to each other. You can list the judge's sentencing options

on the board or flipchart, along with the young person's criminal and family history and anything else that is relevant (such as worries the judge has or statements the young person has made in letters to the judge).
- The leader's role is to let the teens act out the parts and gain some momentum. The actors should engage in a back-and-forth dialogue. However, if the actors get stuck, the leader or the audience can provide prompts or guidance. The leader can also step into one of the roles to provide guidance.
- Tell the group to listen closely to what the characters say and to be ready to discuss the role play when it's over.
- When the scene has played itself out, allow the group to respond. Ask the actors to discuss the emotions they felt while playing their respective characters. Summarize by asking the group if they see the issues faced by the judge or the young person in a new way or have any other reactions.

It's important to debrief after role plays. Otherwise, participants won't have a chance to express feelings that came up.
- We have developed specific role play suggestions for each story. They are available as a free download at the Free Spirit Web site: www.freespirit.com.

Glossary of Legal and Court Terms Used in the Book

AA (Alcoholics Anonymous). A fellowship of men and women whose purpose is to stay sober and help other alcoholics give up drinking. Founded in 1935, over 2 million people belong to AA. The only membership requirement is a desire to stop drinking.

Abuse and neglect. Abuse is physical, emotional, or sexual mistreatment of another. It is a crime and often results in the removal of the child from the home. Neglect is a failure to provide nourishment and care to a child. It may also lead to removal of the child from the home.

Adjusted. A crime is adjusted when it is not formally prosecuted. Instead, the juvenile admits responsibility, receives a punishment, and the case is closed. This keeps some kids from going to court and getting a juvenile record, which could affect his future career. Also called diversion.

Adult court. The court that handles people usually 18 and over who are charged with crimes. Sometimes juveniles are transferred to adult court by the prosecutor or juvenile court judge. Brianne (see section entitled "BRIANNE, 17") was sent to adult court on theft and forgery charges.

Al-Anon. An organization that helps families and friends of alcoholics recover from the effects of living with a problem drinker. There are over 24,000 Al-Anon groups worldwide.

Alateen. An organization of young Al-Anon members, usually teenagers, whose lives are affected by someone else's drinking. Teens share their experiences, discuss their difficulties, encourage one another, and learn effective ways to cope with their problems.

Allege/alleged. To state that something is true before proving it. For example, Adam (see section entitled "ADAM, 15") allegedly threatened to harm other students at his school.

Anger management. Individual or group classes designed to help juveniles control their tempers and avoid criminal behavior (assault, threats, etc.). Andrew (see section entitled "ANDREW, 17") successfully completed anger management classes and has moved on with his life.

Arrest. When the police take a person into custody, usually for breaking a law. The person arrested will be brought before a judge within 48 hours and a decision will be made regarding release or continued jail time.

Attorney. Also called a lawyer, this is a person who is educated in law and licensed by the state to provide legal services, draft legal documents, and represent clients in court.

Charge. When a person is accused of committing a crime, either a charge, citation, complaint, petition, or indictment may be filed against him or her. These are all different ways of accusing someone of breaking the law.

Child protective services. A state agency with the duty to protect children from abuse, neglect, and abandonment. To accomplish this, the child or children may have to be removed from the home and placed in foster care until the problems are resolved.

Cited. When the police give someone who has broken the law a written statement (a ticket or citation). The person must follow the instructions given to him or her, which may include appearing in court.

Community service. Unpaid work the juvenile offender has to do as part of her sentence. There are established programs where the juvenile can do the work, or the juvenile may be allowed to find her own place to work. Schools will often allow the juveniles to do their hours on school grounds, either before or after school or during the lunch period. A failure to do the work may result in further punishment.

Consequence. A consequence is the penalty the court orders after a juvenile admits or is found guilty of a crime. The consequence may include jail time, probation, community service hours, a fine, counseling, and/or payment to the victim.

Corrections officer (CO). An officer who works in a jail or prison.

Counseling/family counseling. Individual, group, or family sessions with a therapist—usually for a number of weeks or months—for the purpose of addressing personal issues such as drug use, anger control, and sexual behavior. A probation officer assists in arranging the counseling and monitoring the juvenile's progress.

Curfew. A law that keeps people (usually minors) from being out on the streets at night. Many cities and towns have juvenile curfews that vary from place to place—check with your local police for the hours in your area.

Custody. When someone has responsibility for another person. In jail, the sheriff has custody of the inmates. In a divorce, a parent has sole or shared custody of the child.

Death sentence/death penalty. Also known as capital punishment. No teen who committed a crime at age 15 or under can receive a death sentence. Some states, however, allow the death penalty for 16- and 17-year-olds.

Deferred jail time. Jail time that is put off to the future. For example, a juvenile court may order a juvenile to spend two weeks in jail at a later date, with the possibility that the teen won't have to do the time if he behaves himself.

Delinquent. A minor who has committed a crime, which is sometimes called a delinquent act.

Detention/detention center. A secure facility that houses juveniles until their court hearings. Juveniles are also sent there after sentencing if the court orders additional jail time.

Dismissal. When the court ends a case without completing it. This usually happens before a trial or sentencing. It can happen for any number of reasons. The prosecutor may not have enough evidence to prove the case, or an important witness or victim can't be located. Sometimes when a case is dismissed, it is refiled at a later date.

Diversion. A process for first-time juvenile offenders who have committed a minor offense (for example, tobacco use, trespassing, truancy, etc.). If the juvenile admits the offense, a punishment is given and formal charges are not filed. This keeps some kids from going to court and getting a juvenile record, which could affect her future career. Generally, if the juvenile fails to complete the punishment, a formal charge or complaint may be filed.

Drug treatment program/drug rehab. A program designed to treat a juvenile who has drug abuse problems. A residential program, where the young person lives on a campus away from home, may last from 30 days to six months. It includes educational classes, individual counseling, peer sessions, role playing, and random drug tests. Most programs offer after-care monitoring to help the juvenile stay clean and sober. A nonresidential program allows the young person to live at home while receiving treatment.

Electronic ankle bracelet. A device usually placed on the juvenile's ankle or arm to keep track of her whereabouts. It triggers a signal to the authorities when the juvenile wearing it goes anywhere other than school, work, or counseling appointments. Depending on the situation, the unit is usually removed after a month of no violations. Removing or tampering with the device may be considered escape.

Felony. A serious crime that is generally punishable by a year or longer in jail.

First-time offender. A juvenile without a previous juvenile record who is now before the court on his first misdemeanor or felony.

Foster care. A licensed home or facility where a child lives after being removed from her home. Foster placement may be temporary or could last for years, depending on the cooperation of the parents in addressing the reasons for removal.

GED. Stands for "general equivalency diploma." It is a diploma earned by studying and passing a series of tests. It is generally available to teens who are 16 or older and who are not attending a formal four-year high school program.

Halfway house. A home in the community where juveniles may live and receive treatment before returning home (usually treatment for drug abuse).

High impact program. A program where a young person spends a brief period in jail, to warn him about his behavior and prevent him from committing crimes. It may last from a few hours to several days. They are also known as "scared straight" programs.

House arrest/house detention. A juvenile placed on house arrest or detention is only allowed to leave the home for school and work. Any other time away from home—doctor's appointments, sports activities, club meetings, etc.—must first be approved by a probation officer. Violations of house detention may result in jail time.

Inmate. A person sentenced to jail or prison. A prisoner.

Judge. The person with the authority under the law to decide cases filed with the court and determine the appropriate penalty.

Juvenile. Any person under age 18 and in the juvenile justice system.

Juvenile awareness program. Also known as a "scared straight" program. A brief visit to prison meant to prevent further criminal behavior. Usually a one-day program, the juvenile meets with adult inmates for a group or one-on-one session. Brandon (see section entitled "BRANDON, 14") attended several juvenile awareness programs at both juvenile and adult prisons.

Juvenile court. A court with the authority to hear and decide cases involving crimes committed by minors, usually people under age 18. A juvenile court also deals with abused, neglected, and abandoned children, and adoptions.

Juvenile detention. A 24-hour secure facility where juveniles live while waiting for their next hearing, or where juveniles serve a jail sentence ordered by the court.

Juvy. An abbreviation for juvenile court, juvenile hall, and juvenile jail.

Life sentence. After being found guilty by a court of certain crimes (for example, murder), a juvenile may be sentenced to spend the rest of his or her life in jail. There are cases in the United States where kids as young as 13 have received a life sentence without the possibility of parole (release). Others have been given a life sentence, but with a chance at being paroled after a number of years.

Mediation/mediator. A process where two or more people who are having a problem sit down with a trained mediator (an expert on problem-solving) to talk about a possible solution. The mediator helps them look at alternatives for handling the situation. Andrew (see section entitled "ANDREW, 17") and his mother participated in mediation before he was released from jail.

MIP class. A class for kids caught drinking or in possession of alcohol or drugs. The class may run for a few hours or a day and involves instruction, videos, individual and group counseling, discussion, and debate on these issues. Natalie (see section entitled "NATALIE, 14") was required to attend a MIP class.

Misdemeanor. A crime that is less serious than a felony and that may result in a fine or up to a year in jail.

NA (Narcotics Anonymous). An international association of recovering drug addicts. NA provides a support network and weekly meetings to help ex-addicts stay clean.

No-contact order. A court order that restricts contact between a juvenile and another person. This may be ordered at someone's request (a victim or parent of a victim) or by the court. For example, a juvenile who is accused of assaulting a kid at school will likely be ordered to have "no contact" with the victim, the victim's family, and any witnesses to the incident. Adam (see section entitled "ADAM, 15") was ordered to have no contact with certain students and witnesses to the threats he made at school. A juvenile may also be ordered to stay away from a boyfriend or girlfriend if the court decides it's in the juvenile's best interests. Starlett (see section entitled "STARLETT, 14") was given such an order regarding her boyfriend. A violation of a no-contact order is a crime and punishable by the court.

Offense. Another word for a crime or when a juvenile has broken the law. Sometimes called a delinquent act.

Parole officer. A juvenile who is sent to jail may be assigned a parole officer for a period of time following his or her release. The parole officer monitors the juvenile's activities for a period of time (parole).

Plea. When a juvenile is charged with a crime, she has to tell the court whether she is guilty or not. This is called a plea. If the juvenile pleads guilty, a sentencing hearing is scheduled. If a not-guilty plea is entered, the case is set for trial. If found guilty of the crime following a trial, the juvenile is then sentenced.

Plea bargain or plea agreement. A process in both juvenile and adult court whereby the state and the defendant (juvenile) agree to a lesser charge in return for the juvenile admitting it. Or the juvenile may agree to admit to one burglary in return for the dismissal of two additional burglaries. Part of the plea agreement may include payment (restitution) to all victims, whether the charges go forward or are dismissed. Plea bargaining is used throughout the criminal justice system to speed cases through crowded courts, to hold juveniles accountable as soon as possible, and to address the victim's rights in a timely manner.

Probation/intensive probation. Probation is when an officer of the court (a probation officer) is assigned to supervise a juvenile for a period of time. This could be from a few months to a year or longer, depending on the person's behavior. The probation officer will be in touch with parents, teachers, employers, and other adults to see how the young person is doing. The purpose of probation is to provide guidance and help when needed. Most kids placed on probation complete their term successfully and are released within a year. Intensive probation is a higher level of supervision for juveniles who need it. It may include daily contact with an assigned probation officer and/or a surveillance officer. It may last for a specific period of time (3 months, 6 months, etc.), after which the juvenile may be reduced to standard probation if he's earned the judge's trust. Violations of intensive probation result in the juvenile going back to court and possibly jail.

Probation officer. A juvenile who is placed on probation by the court is normally assigned a probation officer—an officer of the court who is the judge's eyes and ears in the community regarding the juvenile's activities and compliance with the terms of probation.

Prosecutor. A lawyer who is authorized under the law to file criminal charges against someone and then prosecute or try the case before the court. The prosecutor's job is to prove that you committed the crime that was filed against you. Your defense attorney will argue your side of the story, and the judge or jury will decide the case.

Psychological evaluation. These are conducted by either a court-appointed or private psychologist or psychiatrist. The report is provided to the attorneys in the case and the judge. The report helps identify appropriate services for the juvenile and family.

Psychologist/psychiatrist. A psychologist is an educated and trained professional in the field of human behavior and the mind. A psychiatrist is a physician (a medical doctor) who is a specialist in psychiatry, which deals with the recognition and treatment of mental disorders. Juvenile courts use both psychologists and psychiatrists in evaluating juveniles and making recommendations to the judge regarding treatment and case planning.

Red shirt (also white, blue, and yellow). When a juvenile goes to jail, points are given for good behavior. If the juvenile obeys the rules she gains privileges, such as a later bedtime or participation in gym. Inmates wear shirts of different colors, depending on the level they've reached. They start at the lowest level, wearing a white shirt, and can advance to a blue shirt, then yellow, then red, the highest level. A violation means a loss of points and a return to the lower color shirt. When the juvenile returns to court for her hearing, the judge takes shirt color into consideration in deciding whether to release the juvenile or what kind of sentence to give.

Rehabilitation. To prepare someone who has committed a crime or who is in jail to return to society as a law abiding citizen. A juvenile court is designed to rehabilitate young people, in addition to punishing them.

Residential treatment program/facility. A full-time placement for juveniles away from home, where intensive counseling is available. Kids may stay there from just a few months to several years, depending on their needs. The program is often for juveniles whose behavior problems make it unsafe for them to be at home or in the community.

Restitution. An amount of money paid to the victim of a crime for property loss or damage, or personal injury (medical bills, etc.). Some states allow the juvenile court to order parents of juveniles to pay restitution to the victims for acts committed by their children.

Sentence. The judge's decision in a case regarding the penalty given the juvenile. It may include jail time, probation, community service, a fine, counseling, or additional terms that the judge considers helpful in the juvenile's rehabilitation.

Sentencing. The hearing that is conducted in court to determine the penalty to be given to the juvenile. At the hearing, the prosecutor and defense attorney make recommendations to the judge about the sentence. The victim may also appear and speak to the judge. The juvenile and his or her parents are also present and may make a statement before the judge announces the sentence.

Surveillance officer. An officer of the court who helps supervise juveniles on probation. Surveillance may include coming by your home to check up on you, telephone contact, and personal visits at school and work. The surveillance officer may report violations to the judge, which could result in further hearings.

Therapy. Counseling services with a trained professional to assist juveniles in dealing with problems and issues in their lives.

Trial. A formal hearing in court where the evidence in the case is examined, the law is considered, and a determination is made by the judge or jury. Most of the rights that adults have in a criminal trial are also given to juveniles, including the right to a lawyer, the right to examine witnesses, and the right to remain silent and make the state prove beyond a reasonable doubt that you committed the crime.

Truancy. A truant is a person who is required by state law to go to school (usually a person between ages 6 and 16) and who misses school without a lawful excuse. The school or local prosecutor may take a case of excessive truancy to court. This could result in probation, attendance at a truancy prevention class, or community service.

Urine analysis. A urine test for drugs in your body (also called a drug test or drug screen). The results of the test are given to the attorneys involved, the probation officer, and the judge.

Victim. A person who is harmed by a crime, whether it's a personal crime (assault) or property crime (theft or burglary). A victim has the right to ask to be paid for his or her financial loss, and a juvenile court judge may order the juvenile and parents to pay.

Violation of probation. A person violates his probation when he doesn't obey the rules and procedures of probation. This may be for a technical violation (not checking in with a parole officer) or a substantive violation (committing another crime while on probation). If found guilty of the charge, additional punishment is imposed by the judge.

Warrant. A written court order that authorizes a search of a certain property (car, house, etc.) or an arrest of a named person.

Witness. A person who sees, hears, or knows something about an incident. For example, a witness to a traffic accident may have to come to court and testify about what he or she saw or heard. When Marcus (see section entitled "MARCUS, 14") saw the state's witnesses come into the courtroom at his trial for shoplifting, he changed his mind and decided to plead guilty.

ADAM, 15

a threat made in school

ADAM'S BACKGROUND LEADING UP TO THE CRIME

Adam, 15, is the youngest of four children. His parents are divorced. He lives with his mother, has regular contact with his father, and works part-time in construction for his uncle. Adam earns good grades in school, but has been disciplined a few times for problems with his temper. One day in class, Adam makes a comment to a teacher that he is "homicidal"—wants to kill people. He later says that he was joking and the matter is dropped.

ADAM'S CRIME: SCHOOL INTERFERENCE AND THREATENING

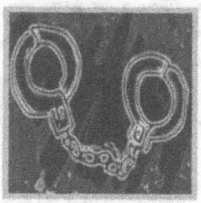

Shortly after the shootings at Columbine High School in Colorado, Adam is in class with a few friends. Other students overhear him talking about the shootings. Adam says that a better way to get rid of kids you don't like is to put sleeping gas in the school vents, and then go through the school and "kill the people you don't like."

Adam is reported to the office, the police are notified, and an investigation is conducted. Adam is brought to court and admits the statement to the prosecutor, but says he was joking. Instead of being charged with the crimes of school interference and threatening, Adam agrees to complete eight community service hours under a diversion program.

For certain crimes, a prosecutor may decide not to file formal charges. Instead, an agreement is reached where the juvenile admits his or her responsibility for the offense and a penalty is decided by the prosecutor. This is called "diversion," because the juvenile is diverted away from formal court proceedings. This speeds cases through the overcrowded courts and prevents a young person from having a criminal record. Diversion is generally available in cases involving minor offenses and a first-time offender. Since Adam did not have a previous juvenile record, he was eligible for the diversion program.

A week after reaching this agreement, Adam gets in a fight with another teen at a party. He is arrested and spends one day in jail before being released to his parents. There isn't enough evidence to determine fault and no charges are filed.

However, because of the fight, the diversion offer is withdrawn by the prosecutor. Two incidents in such a short period of time call for more than community service. Adam is formally charged with school interference and threatening.

He goes to trial and is found guilty of both charges. Now you have to decide what his punishment should be and how to sentence him.

Legal Definitions of School Interference and Threatening

A person commits **INTERFERENCE** with an educational institution by knowingly going upon or remaining upon the property of a school, for the purpose of interfering with the lawful use of such property by others, or in such a manner as to deny or interfere with the lawful use of such property by others.

A person commits **THREATENING** or intimidation if such person threatens or intimidates by word or conduct to cause physical injury to another person, or serious damage to the property of another.

YOUR CONCERNS AS A JUDGE

Adam says he was joking when he threatened to kill kids at school. But can you believe him? There have been a lot of school shootings recently and these kinds of threats have to be taken seriously. Some of the kids who did the shootings talked about it beforehand, but people who overheard didn't do anything about it. Here you have the chance to prevent a possible future tragedy.

There are some positive things in Adam's favor. His parents assure you that they will keep a close eye on him. He has a full-time construction job with his uncle and will be supervised at all times. He will attend night school, with strict hours monitored by his family. You decide to send him home to await sentencing, instead of keeping him in jail.

You receive a recent psychological evaluation on Adam. His tests indicate that he is very intelligent. Adam has also said that he will never go to prison and that he will be very successful someday.

On the other hand, Adam has admitted to trying marijuana on a few occasions. He also has a quick temper and some anti-social traits, as the recent fight shows, and doesn't think he needs treatment or counseling. You are worried that he may act out in an angry way again.

Are the threatening statements at school something to be worried about, or isolated incidents? As a judge, you have to balance what is best for Adam with how to protect the school and community. What about the possibility that Adam makes future threats and acts on them? How should Adam be sentenced?

YOUR SENTENCING OPTIONS AS A JUDGE

The law states that threatening someone with physical injury is a crime. In making your decision, you should consider the kind of threat that was made (such as a bomb threat, a threat to shoot someone, or a threat to beat someone up), and the person's ability to carry through with the threat (there's a difference between threatening to harm someone you know, as opposed to making a threat by email to someone you haven't met). If the person has made more than one threat, and seems to be able to carry it out, the punishment would be harsher.

Sentencing options available to you are:

- Jail time ranging from two weeks to three months, followed by probation for up to one year.

- Jail time ranging from a week to two weeks, along with community service hours, drug testing, counseling, and restricted use of the Internet to prevent him from getting information about weapons, which some kids have done.
- No jail time, but intensive probation from three to six months, which would include daily contacts with a probation officer, with the threat of future jail time of a week to three months if Adam violates his probation terms.
- No jail time, but regular probation for one year, along with community service hours and drug testing.
- Participation in anger management classes and counseling.
- Order Adam to have no contact with his victims and the witnesses against him, such as the person he had a fight with and the kids who reported his threatening comment in school.
- Anything else?

QUESTIONS TO CONSIDER BEFORE SENTENCING ADAM

Write down or discuss your thoughts:
- Do you think Adam was serious about his threat, or do you think he was just fooling around and showing off in front of his friends? Can you answer that question from the evidence, or would you like more information?
- Adam made a previous threat about killing people and got into a recent fight at a party. Is his past history important in making your decision? If so, how? If not, why not?
- Adam is very intelligent, and therefore might have the ability to do something like gas a school. Does this influence the sentence you give him?

- Does the fact that Adam smokes marijuana concern you? Does that influence his sentence? Why or why not?
- Adam served a day in jail after he got into the fight. Should he be given any more jail time? If so, how much? If not, why not?
- Should Adam get help for his anger? Should he be required to attend group counseling with peers, individual counseling, or family counseling? Or all three?
- Adam says he doesn't need counseling. Should you order him to participate anyway? Will he get anything out of counseling if he doesn't want to be there?
- Is there any additional information you would like about Adam to help you make your decision? If so, what is it and why would it help you make your decision?

YOU BE THE JUDGE

Complete this sentence:
Based on the information available to me, Adam's sentence should be...

WHAT ACTUALLY HAPPENED

When the day arrived for Adam's sentencing, he was going to school, earning A's and B's, and working with his uncle. I agonized over how to sentence him. I knew that I was seeing Adam and his family for only brief periods in court, when most people are on their best behavior. I also knew that because of his high intelligence, Adam had the ability to carry through on his threat of gassing the school and killing students. I had to strike a balance between what was best for Adam and how to protect the school and community.

I worried that whatever I decided would be either too harsh or too easy on him. On the one hand, I didn't think a long period of jail time was necessary. On the other hand, I didn't feel that the one day he spent in jail for the fight was enough. I wanted to give Adam the message that the community takes verbal threats seriously. I sentenced Adam to a combination of jail time and probation that would also include community service, counseling, and drug testing.

- He was ordered to spend his upcoming spring break, a total of nine days, in jail. I told Adam that he should spend this time reflecting on what landed him there and how he planned to continue with his life.
- He was allowed to continue living with his aunt and uncle but was required to complete 100 hours of community service.
- Because Adam had admitted earlier that he tried marijuana on a few occasions, I also required that he be tested for drugs during probation.

- He was required to attend individual counseling to address his anger and self-control issues.
- He was ordered to stay off the Internet while on probation (assuming the worst, I didn't want Adam to have easy access to information about weapons).

As I watched Adam and his family leave the courtroom, I hoped I wouldn't see him again or read about him in the news-paper. Part of me worried that I might.

YOUR RESPONSE TO THE JUDGE'S DECISION

Write down or discuss your thoughts:
- Are you surprised by the judge's sentence? Why or why not?
- Was it harder or easier on Adam than your sentence? In what ways?

- What part of the judge's sentence do you agree with? What part do you disagree with? Why?
- Do you think Adam's statement in school was blown out of proportion and that he was punished too severely? Or do you think his sentence was right under the circumstances? Why?
- What do you think will happen to Adam?

Letter from Adam While Serving His Jail Sentence (age 16)

Your Honor,
Thank you for giving me this chance to speak on my behalf. I never intended anything by my remark. It was a stupid comment and I am terribly sorry that it came to this. The whole thing started in third period after the Columbine incident. The discussion had come up repeatedly in class. While the class was just small talking, I mentioned to my friend off the top of my head that the best way to do it, if it was

physically possible, which it's not, is to put sleeping gas in the vents and then go through and kill the people you didn't like. I know I shouldn't have said something like that because that's like commenting on a bomb or a gun in the airport. People take those comments seriously, now I understand that. Everyone makes mistakes and boy have I made a lot of mistakes. I am going to acquire a G.E.D. and attend community college for an associates degree in drafting. Basically who I was five months or so ago I had to drop, I have had to grow up, I can't goof around anymore. I have to get things done and make a way for myself.

    Sincerely,
    Adam

ADAM TODAY

Adam successfully completed one year of probation and was released just before his 18th birthday. He stayed with his aunt and uncle for another six months and then returned to his father's home. He earned his GED and worked at a fitness center. He is now 19 and attending college as a psychology major. He has a brown belt in martial arts and is thinking of joining the military. He also works part-time as a loan officer at a mortgage company.

Adam never thought a casual conversation with friends could be overheard and misinterpreted. Of course, the question is whether his comments were misinterpreted or interpreted correctly. Only Adam knows the answer to this. He learned a valuable lesson as a teenager—words alone may have serious consequences.

FINAL THOUGHTS

Write down or discuss your thoughts:
- What was your reaction to Adam's letter from jail? Did it change your view of his actions or his sentence? Why or why not?
- Have you ever heard anyone at school or work make a comment like Adam's? Did the comment worry you? Could you tell if the person was serious or not? What, if anything, did you do?
- Do you feel you have a responsibility to report someone who makes those kinds of comments? Why or why not?
- Have you ever wanted to get even with someone? How did you handle the temptation? Looking back now, are you happy with the way you handled it? Why or why not?

- When you get angry, how do you deal with your feelings? Do you talk with your parents or a friend, or just let it build up? Do you have a school counselor, a trusted adult, or a friend you can talk to? What could you do to deal with your feelings?

Did You Know?

- Every day, 135,000 children bring a gun to school.
- The Wisconsin Supreme Court ruled in 2001 that a student's creative writing assignment, in which he described cutting off his teacher's head, was protected by the First Amendment (In re Douglas D., 243 Wis.2d 204).
- On the other hand, Massachusetts decided that the drawing of a student pointing a gun at his teacher constituted a threat and was not constitutionally protected (Commonwealth v. Milo M., 433 Mass. 149 [2001]).

ADELINA, 13

robbing a girl

ADELINA'S BACKGROUND LEADING UP TO THE CRIME

Adelina comes from a large family. She has six brothers and sisters, ranging in age from a toddler to a 17-year-old. She lives with her mother and stepfather and does not know her father. The family is poor and because of the number of younger children to care for, her parents have little control over Adelina and her older siblings. Adelina manipulates her mother to get what she wants and has basically no relationship with her stepfather.

When Adelina finishes the 8th grade, her older brother gets involved in gang trouble and her older sister is charged with aggravated assault. Both are put on probation. Adelina is not a gang member, but knows her brother's friends and is considered a "gang wannabe" by the police.

Her criminal history begins when she's only 11. She and a friend are caught in a Wal-Mart store taking cosmetics. The next month Adelina hits a girl at school, and she is charged with shoplifting and assault. She admits to the shoplifting and the assault charge is dismissed. Adelina is put on probation and ordered to take a class on teens and the law, which she completes. She is also ordered to complete a four-hour jail-prevention program for young, first-time offenders (kids who have never been to jail before). This half-day program includes a tour of a jail and a discussion with some of the inmates. Adelina attends this program and returns home.

After four months on probation, Adelina gets caught with the same friend shoplifting again. They take school supplies, jewelry, and some shirts. Adelina not only admits stealing, but also admits to her probation officer that she is a gang member and that she's tried alcohol and marijuana. As a result, she is kept on probation and one of her new probation terms requires that she be tested for drugs. She does fine for two months, until one of her tests comes back positive for marijuana. Adelina admits she's been smoking pot on a weekly basis. She's required to have drug counseling and her activities are more closely monitored by her probation officer, who makes both face-to-face and phone contact.

ADELINA'S CRIME: ROBBERY

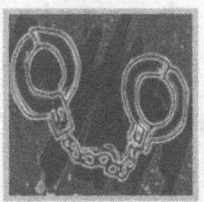

Three months after she tests positive for marijuana use, Adelina and a friend beat up a girl, steal some of her things, including a pager, and flee the scene. Adelina, now 13, is charged with robbery and admits to a lesser charge of theft in a plea bargain. (Robbery is a more serious crime because it's committed against a person. Theft or burglary involves stealing something without a person being around.) Because the victim couldn't say for sure who hit her, Adelina isn't charged with assault. Adelina remains in jail for 30 days until she appears before you for sentencing.

When someone is accused of a crime, a prosecutor may decide to lower the offense charged (in this case, from the more serious charge of robbery to the less serious charge of theft) if the juvenile is willing to admit to the lesser charge. This is called a plea bargain and happens often. Plea bargaining holds the juvenile accountable for an offense through a guilty plea, and results in a quicker end to the case by avoiding a more lengthy trial.

Legal Definition of Theft

A person commits **THEFT** if, without lawful authority, the person

> knowingly controls property of another, with the intent to deprive the other person of such property, or comes into control of lost, mislaid, or misdelivered property of another under circumstances providing means of inquiry as to the true owner, and appropriates such property to the person's own or another person's use, without reasonable efforts to notify the true owner.

YOUR CONCERNS AS A JUDGE

It was almost a year ago that you placed Adelina on probation for the shoplifting and the assault at school. She stands before you again, charged with a serious offense. She has been involved in two shoplifting incidents, a robbery, and at least one assault. She is also in a gang and using drugs. And she's only 13 years old, about to turn 14.

You arrange for her to meet with a psychologist because she has never been evaluated before. You want suggestions to help her turn her life around. The doctor tells you that Adelina's reasoning ability is good, that she is sorry about the illegal things she has done, and claims that God is her strength and the answer to her prayers.

The psychologist recommends that Adelina be placed in a residential treatment facility specializing in drug treatment. He tells you that if Adelina is not able to stop using drugs and stay away from gangs, jail may be the only alternative.

Adelina admits to you in court and in a letter (see box entitled "Letter from Adelina While in Jail Awaiting Sentencing (age 14)") that she has a serious drug abuse problem. She says that drugs help her escape her pain. She has admitted using crack, cocaine, marijuana, and alcohol, and has also sniffed paint. She says she can't stay away from drugs because they're so easily available and all her friends do drugs. Now that she's in jail awaiting sentencing, she is asking for help.

How can you help Adelina? Does she need punishment, help getting off drugs, or both?

YOUR SENTENCING OPTIONS AS A JUDGE

Even though Adelina pled guilty to theft through a plea bargain, you can take into account that she committed a crime against a person. When that happens, probation is usually ordered, with additional punishment depending on the case. In Adelina's case, she was already on probation with a growing number of offenses. Therefore, a stricter penalty may be in order. Your options for Adelina are:

• Jail time for six to twelve months.

- Jail time for six months or less, with continued probation for up to one year.
- Placement in foster care temporarily, while you do more research on Adelina's home situation.
- Placement in a residential treatment program with counseling for drug abuse.
- Intensive probation, where Adelina is monitored on a daily basis for six months with strict terms, including counseling at home for drug abuse.
- One month of house arrest, individual and family counseling, drug treatment and testing, payment to the victim for the pager, and future jail time if she doesn't follow her probation terms.
- Regular probation for up to one year, with counseling at home.
- Payment to the victim and close the case.
- Anything else?

Letter from Adelina While in Jail Awaiting Sentencing (age 14)

Dear Judge Jacobs,

I bet you're not too happy to see my face again, and I'm not too happy to be here myself. The reason why I am writing is to apologize to you for what I've done. I know I've said it so many times, but truly, from my heart, I regret what I've done this time. I've got too many problems for a 14-year-old. I have to admit that drugs is one of them. I want to change my life around, but I know actions speak louder than words. I hope you think this too and give me that last chance. I know if you do, you won't regret it.

Thank you.
Adelina

QUESTIONS TO CONSIDER BEFORE SENTENCING ADELINA

Write down or discuss your thoughts:
- Adelina admits having a drug problem. She won't stay home or listen to her parents. She's in a gang and has little respect for authority. She is committing more frequent and serious crimes. How would you handle her case, based on her history? What would help Adelina turn her life around?
- Do you trust sending Adelina home, to once again try to behave? Why or why not?
- Should you give Adelina additional jail time? Or are the 30 days she's already served awaiting sentencing enough?

- Adelina's parents have little control over her and her older siblings are involved in crime. Is Adelina's family part of the problem or the cause of some of her behaviors? If so, what can be done with her family if you let her return home?
- Drugs are easy to get in Adelina's neighborhood and her friends are a bad influence. Would you consider removing her from her home into foster care? If so, why and for how long? If not, why not?
- What about Adelina being in a gang? What do you do about that?
- Do you think Adelina is running away from her problems? What could be done to help her face them, rather than run away?
- What is your reaction to Adelina's letter? Does it affect the sentence you give her? Why or why not?
- Do you think Adelina's request for help is sincere? Why or why not? What does she need help with the most?

YOU BE THE JUDGE

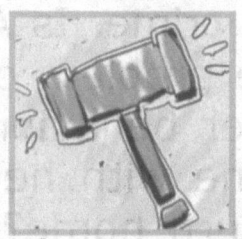

Complete this sentence:
Based on the information available to me, Adelina's sentence should be...

WHAT ACTUALLY HAPPENED

Adelina's court date finally arrived. She had a few discipline problems while in jail, but for the most part controlled her temper.

At the hearing, I explained to her what was recommended by the psychologist who reviewed her case. I told her that I agreed that residential placement in a drug treatment program would give her the best chance of returning to her family and having a successful future. But due to a lack of funding, there weren't any beds available in the various programs, so I was unable to place Adelina in a program right away. It would be three to six months before a spot might open up for her.

> Judges have to work with the money and programs available to them. A teenager like Adelina may need multiple services, but the judge may be limited in what he or she can order. Because of this, judges are often frustrated in their attempts to help teens and their families.

While in jail, Adelina did not receive the services she needed because juvenile jails are generally meant for short-term stays—there's not enough time to complete a drug treatment program, for example. However, some help could be arranged for her at home if she were released, as long as she cooperated and stayed put. I explained that she was being released that day to go home, and immediately placed her on intensive probation, where she would be monitored on a daily basis for the next six months. I told Adelina that she might end up back in jail if she

didn't work on her issues and follow her probation terms, as follows:
- One month of house arrest—Adelina could leave the house only for school and counseling appointments.
- Participation in individual and family counseling.
- Completion of a substance abuse program, including drug testing, while living at home.
- Payment of $35 to the victim for the pager.
- Follow all juvenile laws, including keeping a curfew, not running away, going to school, and no cigarette smoking.
- I also sentenced Adelina to an additional 30 days in jail in the future, but only if she messed up on any of these terms. If she behaved herself, I wouldn't have to lock her up again.

YOUR RESPONSE TO THE JUDGE'S DECISION

Write down or discuss your thoughts:
- Are you surprised by the judge's sentence? Why or why not?
- Was it harder or easier on Adelina than your sentence? In what ways?
- What part of the judge's sentence do you agree with? What part do you disagree with? Why?
- What part of this sentence do you think will be hardest for Adelina to follow? Why?
- What part of this sentence will be most helpful to Adelina? Why?
- Is there anything left out of the judge's decision that you would have included? What is it, and why would you have included it?

- The judge's first choice was to put Adelina in a drug treatment facility away from home, but there weren't any spaces available for her. Are you surprised there weren't enough spaces available? What is your reaction to this?
- Will Adelina follow her probation terms? Why or why not?

ADELINA AFTER SENTENCING

Following her release, Adelina stayed out of trouble for about six months. She paid the robbery victim from baby-sitting money, went to school and counseling, and her drug tests were clean.

But then she was caught using drugs again. She spent an additional two weeks in jail and was put back on intensive probation.

Throughout this period, various resources were available to Adelina and her family—home therapy, family counseling, and a "scared straight" program (also known as a juvenile awareness program), where Adelina visited a state women's prison to hear inmates talk about being locked up. She was also required to wear an electronic ankle bracelet that monitored her whereabouts.

Adelina cut off the bracelet and ran away. She was gone for three months before she was arrested on a warrant. Back in jail again, Adelina tested positive for marijuana, speed, and cocaine.

A space in a long-term residential treatment facility never became available for Adelina. And I never considered a short-term (30- or 60-day) program for her, given her heavy use of drugs and criminal history.

While in jail this time, Adelina assaulted another inmate. She was obviously out of control. Despite all the chances she had been given, she was a danger to herself and others, and needed a long-term, secure environment. I had little choice but to send her to jail for a minimum of six months—her release after would depend on her behavior. While in jail, she would be placed in a drug treatment program.

I explained to Adelina my reasons for sending her to jail. She had used up everything the juvenile justice system had to offer. After years of services and monitoring by the court system, I was ready to throw up my hands in frustration.

I told her that, contrary to what she might think, going to jail was not "The End." I was not giving up on her. This was just the final step in the juvenile process—a long-term punishment meant to make a difference in her life before she reached adulthood. I told her I would keep track of her progress, and encouraged her to use her time in jail to plan her future. She had total control over what that future might be.

ADELINA TODAY

Adelina is now 16 and remains in jail. She has not had an easy time during her stay, but continues to try to do her best. She knows that she could earn her release on parole, or that she may stay in jail until she turns 18. For the most part, the choice is hers.

Adelina doesn't know why she had so much trouble giving up drugs. She said she'll be happy when she's "back with her family and sober." She knows she "could have a better life without drugs—I feel proud when I'm sober and smiling."

FINAL THOUGHTS

Write down or discuss your thoughts:
- Were you surprised that Adelina continued to do drugs and get into trouble? Why or why not?
- Do you think it would have made a difference if Adelina had been sent to a long-term residential drug treatment center away from home? Why or why not?
- One of Adelina's problems was that she couldn't stay away from gang

members. Have you ever been told by your parents to stay away from someone? Did you do it? If you ever saw a younger sibling with someone you didn't like, what would you do?
- Do you know anyone who has stolen something or is tempted to shoplift? Would you say anything to that person?
- Do you know anyone who has a drug problem? What kind of help do people need to give up drugs?
- Do you think Adelina will someday straighten out her life? Why or why not? What does she need to do to get her problems under control?

Did You Know?

- In 2000, 26,800 juveniles were arrested for robbery: 91 percent were boys, 27 percent were under age 15.
- Thirty-two percent of students report that they have been offered, sold, or given an illegal drug at school in the last year.
- Incidents of physical attack, robbery, and bullying at school

increase significantly with the pressure of drug dealers at school.

(Office of Juvenile Justice and Delinquency Prevention, Statistical Briefing Book 2002)

ANDREW, 17

a fight with a brother

ANDREW'S BACKGROUND LEADING UP TO THE CRIME

When Andrew is 15, his parents get divorced. His father remarries shortly after and moves out of state, while Andrew and his brother, who is three years older, stay with their mother. Most of the time Andrew gets along with his brother, but occasionally they get into a fight and hit each other. More than once, Andrew ends up in a hospital emergency room needing stitches.

As a result of his family's breakup, Andrew becomes depressed. He continues to go to school, where he's in gifted programs, but he loses his temper more often and is generally mad at the world. He takes anti-depressant medication, sees a counselor, and goes to anger management classes.

ANDREW'S CRIME: DOMESTIC VIOLENCE

When Andrew is 17, he gets into a fight with his brother and the matter is referred to juvenile court. Before Andrew can appear in court, he's at home one night with his girlfriend, mother, and brother. An argument starts over something minor and Andrew's brother pushes his girlfriend. Andrew comes to her defense and gets in between the two. The situation gets out of control. Andrew grabs a knife and scissors and lunges at his brother. No one is hurt but the police are called to the house. They question Andrew, place him under arrest, and take him to jail. He is charged with domestic violence and admits to the crime. Sentencing is to take place in 30 days.

When a suspect admits to a crime, sentencing usually takes place two to four weeks later. If the suspect pleads not guilty, a trial is scheduled to begin within a month or so, depending on whether the suspect is released or remains in jail awaiting trial.

Legal Definition of Domestic Violence

DOMESTIC VIOLENCE means any act that violates certain designated laws, including disorderly conduct and assault, if the victim and the defendant are related by blood, adoption, or marriage.

YOUR CONCERNS AS A JUDGE

You first meet Andrew in court the day after he's arrested and brought to jail. As you speak to him and his mother, you notice that he seems sorry about what happened and even in shock. Andrew doesn't fit the profile of most kids in jail. He is not committing crimes in the neighborhood. He isn't in a gang, using drugs, or running away. He is a law-abiding teen who's in gifted programs in school and holds a job. This isn't the typical juvenile case, except for the fact that Andrew can't control his temper. He does not come across as an angry person, but does admit that the situation at home is sometimes tense.

His mother doesn't think that sending him home is the best thing.

You explain to them that a cooling-off period seems like the wisest choice.

Although Andrew wants to go home right away, you tell him that a mediation meeting will be scheduled in a day or so and that he is going to stay in jail until then. Andrew doesn't like it, but he agrees to do his best. You explain the purpose of mediation—that a trained professional will sit down with him and his mother (and possibly his brother) to discuss the future. Since Andrew's brother hasn't been charged with a crime, you don't have legal control over him, and you can't require him to attend mediation, but you tell Andrew and his mother that you would like the brother to attend the mediation and, later on, Andrew's sentencing.

> In mediation, two or more people who have a dispute (like Andrew and his brother) try to reach an agreement with the assistance of a neutral mediator. If an agreement is reached, it is sent to the judge for approval. The judge may ask for changes in the agreement before approving it. The

advantages of mediation are quick conflict resolution and avoiding the ordeal of going to trial.

Mediation in criminal cases, including juvenile delinquents, is a growing trend. In 2002, 12-year-old Alex and 13-year-old Derek were convicted by a jury in Florida of starting a fire and murder. They killed their father with a baseball bat while he was sleeping and set the house on fire. They were facing 20 years to life in prison. Because of misconduct by the prosecutor during their trial, the guilty verdicts were thrown out and the judge ordered mediation to try to resolve the case. As a result, the boys pled guilty to a lesser offense and were sentenced to seven and eight years in prison.

Andrew and his mother meet with the court mediator. They reach an agreement—Andrew agrees to attend counseling, stop smoking cigarettes, and not possess any weapons, including knives. He is also prohibited from being left alone with his brother. Andrew's mother says she will take him home as long as he obeys this agreement. Andrew signs the agreement to get out of jail.

While in jail, another inmate grabbed Andrew and held a sharpened spoon to his neck, leaving a red mark. Andrew now wants out of jail in the worst way. You approve the mediation agreement. After four days in jail, he goes home with his mother.

The fight with his brother could have had a tragic ending, and Andrew realizes this. But are the terms of the mediation agreement enough to make sure Andrew isn't violent again? Or should the court take additional action? What, if anything, can be done to help Andrew stay calm and not lose his temper in stressful situations?

YOUR SENTENCING OPTIONS AS A JUDGE

In sentencing a person guilty of domestic violence, the relationship and ages of the people involved are important, as well as the frequency of the violence. Is it an assault by a parent on a child or a fight between siblings? Is it a one-time incident, or have there been numerous assaults between family members? Different cases require different approaches, depending on the kind of violence. Jail may be an option depending on the nature of the case, and probation is almost always required.

Sentencing options available to you are:
- A jail sentence ranging from one to four weeks.
- Send Andrew to live with a relative for a while, or place him in foster care temporarily, while he receives individual and family counseling to prepare him to return to the family.
- Probation for one year, with the threat of future jail time if there are any new offenses.
- Probation with continued counseling for anger and depression, along with anger management classes,

and require Andrew to write a report about what he learned.
- No probation, with credit for the four days already served.
- Anything else?

QUESTIONS TO CONSIDER BEFORE SENTENCING ANDREW

Write down or discuss your thoughts:
- Is the mediation agreement enough? Or should Andrew be given additional time in jail before being sent home?
- If you send Andrew home, what additional safety measures would you put into place to prevent fights?
- Should Andrew go to a relative's home or into a foster home temporarily? Or is this the type of

situation that Andrew, his mother, and his brother can work out?
- What about Andrew's brother? There's no guarantee they won't be left alone together. The brother couldn't be forced to attend mediation. If the brother comes to Andrew's sentencing, what would you say to him?
- What about Andrew's anger and depression over his parents' divorce? Should the court try to help him cope with that anger and depression? If so, how? If not, why not?
- Is a court only supposed to punish crime? Or should the court try to help people with the personal and family problems that may have caused them to commit crime? Why or why not?

YOU BE THE JUDGE

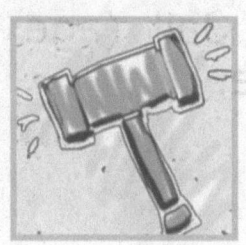

Complete this sentence:
Based on the information available to me, Andrew's sentence should be...

WHAT ACTUALLY HAPPENED

I considered the four days that Andrew already served in jail to be enough of a wake-up call. I placed Andrew on probation for one year and told him to complete the counseling and anger management classes. His mother was in court and I told her she had to exercise better control over her sons and participate in Andrew's counseling. I told them they both had to work hard to avoid further police and court involvement. Andrew knew he had to control his temper and learn better ways to deal with his anger. I also required him to write a report about what he learned from his experience in jail (see section entitled "Report from Andrew About Jail (age 17)"). Then I sent him home.

YOUR RESPONSE TO THE JUDGE'S DECISION

Write down or discuss your thoughts:
- Are you surprised by the judge's sentence? Why or why not?
- Was it harder or easier on Andrew than your sentence? In what ways?
- What part of the judge's sentence do you agree with? What part do you disagree with? Why?
- Is there anything missing from the judge's sentence? If so, why is it important?
- Do you think Andrew will stay out of fights with his brother? Why or why not?
- What should be done if Andrew is violent again?

Report from Andrew About Jail (age 17)

Lessons Learned

From my trip through the juvenile justice system, I have learned many things.

First, I learned that I have an anger problem. I went to the anger management classes, but I still have a long way to go. I still get angry, but I don't hit or throw anything. Now I just leave the situation. I need to be at a point where the little things don't upset me, but for the time being I have learned how to control my temper.

Second, I have a lot to be thankful for in life—my family, my dog, my cats, and my friends. Having all of the important things in my life taken from me has made me appreciate all the things in life that I took for granted—my car, my freedom, and my mom. Being taken away from my mom was so painful for me because I saw how much it hurt my mother. I took my mother's feelings for granted. I still feel incredibly bad for all the turmoil I put my mother through, and I will probably feel horrible about what I did for the rest of my life. I learned that my brother cares about me, a lot more than I thought he did. I am going to have to live with the fact that I could have seriously hurt my brother over nothing, and that scares me. I learned who were my real friends and who weren't. My real friends cared about me and were concerned. The others just thought it was funny.

Third, I have learned that my life was running me instead of me running it. My life was in utter chaos, and is now starting to turn around, slowly but surely. I have a job, I am not slacking off in school, I am going to class. And most importantly, I am listening to my mom, whether it be advice or instruction. I ended my relationship with my girlfriend. She was leading me down a path to nowhere and taking me away from my family. But most importantly, I feel that I have direction in my life. I have a plan for what I want to do. I want to go to college and go into medicine for a career. I made the decision to do my homework and to try my hardest in school.

Lastly, I have learned that violence is never acceptable. I never thought that this would happen to me. When I was young my brother would regularly send me to the emergency room for stitches, or would regularly beat me up, so from a very young age I have learned that violence can hurt people, but nothing reinforced that more than the look on my mother's face as the police car pulled away with me in the back. I still remember the exact expression on my mom's face when the police officer said that I was being arrested. The feeling of how much you have hurt someone who cares about you, of

> *how much pain they are feeling, is the worst feeling in the world. Seeing my mother cry because of me was like someone just ripping my heart out. The feeling is just unexplainable.*
> *Andrew*

ANDREW TODAY

Andrew obeyed his terms and was successfully released from probation two months before his 18th birthday.

Andrew is now 20 and studying psychology in college. He is an assistant manager at a video store, where he has worked for the past two years. He lives at home and reports that his relationship with his brother has improved. With their busy schedules, they hardly see each other. Andrew is a film buff, and when time allows he works with stained glass. His goal is to earn a doctorate in psychology.

Andrew represents the majority of kids who get a taste of what it's like to be in jail. Although it was a brief stay, the impact was great. Andrew was not a criminal or a teen with anti-social tendencies. He simply lost his temper and reacted. Like many who come before the court, a jolt of reality—that there are consequences for misbehavior—was all that was necessary to get his attention. Andrew will likely turn this experience into something useful as he works with future clients as a psychologist.

FINAL THOUGHTS

- What is your reaction to the report Andrew wrote about jail? Are you surprised by anything he said?
- How do you handle conflicts with siblings or parents? What, if anything, would you like to change

about the way conflicts are handled in your family?
- If your parents are divorced, how did that experience affect you? How do you deal with the feelings that come up?
- What are some appropriate ways to let off steam when you get angry? What are some things you might choose to not do when you lose your temper?

Did You Know?

Over 3 million kids are exposed each year to domestic violence in their homes. One million women each year, most between ages 16 and 24, and an average of 160,000 males each year, are victims of domestic violence (Department of Justice Study 2000).

ASHLEY, 14

caught with a bag of marijuana

ASHLEY'S BACKGROUND LEADING UP TO THE CRIME

Ashley's parents divorce when she's 2. Because her parents have joint custody, she has regular contact with both her mother and father. Both parents work and have remarried. She lives primarily with her mother and two younger brothers.

Ashley has a difficult relationship with her mother because she was left in charge of her brothers for days at a time while her mother worked. When she returned to school, she had to catch up on what she missed. She feels neglected, yet craves her mother's attention. Her mother was also suspected of using drugs when Ashley was a child, but there's no evidence she uses drugs now and she says she's clean.

Ashley starts using drugs when she's 12 and in the 8th grade. She first tries alcohol and marijuana, and soon becomes a regular user. She also experiments with LSD and then crystal meth, which becomes her drug of choice. Her parents are unaware that Ashley is using drugs.

By age 14, Ashley's behavior is dangerous and destructive. When she goes to school she gets A's and B's, but she also breaks curfew, cuts school a lot, runs away from home from time to time, and continues to do drugs.

ASHLEY'S CRIME: POSSESSION OF MARIJUANA

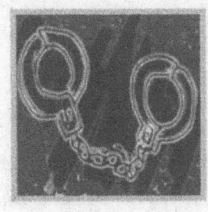

Ashley's mother finds a baggie of marijuana in her dresser drawer. When confronted by her parents with the evidence, Ashley admits that it's hers. They take Ashley and the marijuana to the police station, where she again admits to possessing and using the drug. She says she doesn't think there's anything wrong with it and plans to continue to smoke. She is sent home to await sentencing.

Legal Definition of Possession of Marijuana

A person shall not knowingly **POSSESS OR USE MARIJUANA,** which means all parts of any plant of the genus cannabis.

YOUR CONCERNS AS A JUDGE

Ashley's juvenile record previously consisted of curfew violations, truancy, and a few runaway incidents. But now she is before you on a marijuana charge. And you can't ignore a drug history of experimenting with LSD, crystal meth, and alcohol, which she freely admits.

Ashley knows her way of dealing with her feelings and frustrations is to use drugs. Although she said before that there is nothing wrong with smoking marijuana, you know from her probation reports that she now understands she has a problem and is asking for help. She is aware that probation means that she will be supervised and that any violation could result in being locked up. Ashley's behavior over the past year shows that she has a defiant attitude and does whatever she pleases.

Is there something other than jail or probation that would help Ashley deal with her issues? Since she now wants to stop using but can't do it on her own, is jail the only alternative?

YOUR SENTENCING OPTIONS AS A JUDGE

Ordinarily, when a teenager is charged with truancy and runaway offenses, you would issue a warning and order a few counseling sessions. But when drugs enter the picture, it's time to take a closer look at what's going on. It's important to find out if the drug use is a onetime incident or whether the teen is a regular user. Since Ashley has an extensive history of drug use from a young age, she needs some form of supervision and treatment.

Sentencing options available to you are:
- Jail time ranging from one to three months, including a drug treatment program while in jail to make sure all drugs are out of her system,

with probation for one year after release.
- Placement in a residential drug treatment program away from home, followed by probation.
- Probation for one year with participation in a drug awareness class while she lives at home, drug testing, and family counseling.
- No court-ordered drug treatment, leaving it up to the family to arrange, but probation with the threat of future jail time if Ashley starts using drugs again, and attendance at a drug awareness class commonly referred to as MIP (Minor in Possession) class.
- Anything else?

QUESTIONS TO CONSIDER BEFORE SENTENCING ASHLEY

Write down or discuss your thoughts:
- Would you order Ashley to spend time in jail? Why or why not?
- In your opinion, does jail time stop young people from using drugs again? Is jail the best way to deal with drug offenses? Why or why not?
- Does Ashley need to be punished? Or does she just need help in overcoming her drug dependence? Or both?
- Ashley's parents say that they're concerned about Ashley's welfare and will do anything to help her. Yet they say they're completely unaware of her heavy drug use. She loves her parents, but has little respect for them. She feels neglected by her mother, yet craves her attention. What changes in the parents' behavior would you like to see? How would you go about helping the family?
- Ashley's own mother supposedly used drugs, and now Ashley is before the court on a drug charge. Should Ashley's mother be held

partly responsible for her daughter's behavior? If so, how? If not, why not?

YOU BE THE JUDGE

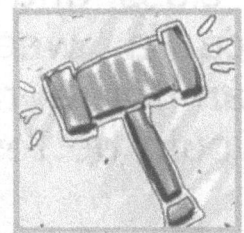

Complete this sentence:
   Based on the information available to me, Ashley's sentence should be...

WHAT ACTUALLY HAPPENED

Ashley showed up at her sentencing with her parents and step-parents. They were cooperative and very concerned about their daughter. Ashley said she wanted help and was willing to try staying at home, in school, and off drugs. I didn't see a need right then to lock her up, but I told Ashley that jail was a possibility if she got into any more trouble. I gave her the following sentence:

- She was placed on probation for up to one year.
- She was ordered to participate in family counseling with her parents.
- She was required to attend a drug awareness class and be tested for drugs twice a week. If Ashley stayed clean for a month or two, then she would be tested only once a week.

I told Ashley that a bed in jail was available for her, but I hoped we wouldn't have to use it.

YOUR RESPONSE TO THE JUDGE'S DECISION

Write down or discuss your thoughts:
- Are you surprised by the judge's sentence? Why or why not?
- Was it harder or easier on Ashley than your sentence? In what ways?

- What part of the judge's sentence do you agree with? What part do you disagree with? Why?
- Is there anything missing from the judge's decision? What is it, and why do you think it's important?
- What do you predict will happen to Ashley?

ASHLEY AFTER SENTENCING

Ashley soon started using drugs again. She was offered services to help turn her life around. She went to drug treatment programs, as well as to several "high impact" programs that were conducted in jail for three to four days at a time, to make a bigger impression on her.

Each time she violated probation she got more penalties. She completed "Life Sentence," a class conducted by mothers of teens who were killed by acts of violence. I thought Ashley might decide to stop using drugs if she heard from these mothers. In fact, Ashley liked the program so much she attended a second time on her own.

She also was placed on house arrest, where she was allowed out of the house only for school, drug testing, and counseling. After she ran away again, she was required to wear an electronic ankle bracelet so her whereabouts could be monitored.

However, she kept doing drugs and running away. At one point Ashley was missing for eight days before a hospital emergency room called her mother and said she was there for an overdose. She spent 17 days in jail before being released to her parents. This was the longest period that she had ever been locked up.

Letter from Ashley While in Jail (age 15)

Judge Jacobs,
I want to take the time to write you a letter, to give you some insight on my situation. First of all, I wanted you to know that I have realized how important my family is to me since I've been in jail. I now know that doing drugs and being away from home was

slowly but surely killing me. My parents were so worried, and now I know. I just want to go home so I can be with people who love me, instead of being with people who really don't care for me at all. I would be so grateful to have just one final chance to prove I can be trusted. I pray that on the 19th, my court date, I can be released to my mother, who wants me home as bad as I want to go. I look at my reflection in the mirror, and see empty eyes. I do not regret my mistakes, sir, I only learn and move on. I know I can be that awesome honor roll kid again, who's been dying to come out for years. I just ask that I am given one more chance. If I mess up again, I expect to be locked up for good. I am comfortable with that. I hope to be home with family for Christmas.

Sincerely,
Ashley

Ashley always believed that neither one of her parents loved her or wanted her. She always felt that her mom wanted to push her off on her dad, and that her dad did the same. Oddly enough, the relationship between Ashley and her parents improved while she was in jail. Her parents visited her regularly. They opened up to each other and Ashley began to accept the fact that both of her parents loved her. Unfortunately, they were clueless about the pain that led to Ashley's drug use.

ASHLEY TODAY

Ashley is out of jail now, on probation, and lives with her father and stepmother. She maintains regular contact with her mother. She is participating in family therapy with her parents. Her random drug tests have been clean for the past year. She is back in school and hopes to be the first in her family to graduate from college.

Ashley plans to become a dental hygienist. She just started her first job and works part-time as a clerk at a grocery store. She recently sent me this letter:

Letter from Ashley

Judge Jacobs,

I should probably start by telling you that I am grateful for your compassion near the holidays. I know I appreciate my life a thousand times more than I used to. I will never forget my experience in jail. My stay there was hardly pleasant. All I could think about was my family. I also thought about small things that never crossed my mind until I was locked up. Even having soda or going to a fast-food restaurant seemed like a luxury to me. I am really sorry that I have wasted so much of my time, as well as other people's time. While in jail, I had not realized how many people honestly care about me. So many of my family, teachers, and friends of the family wanted to visit me. Everyone was so concerned with my life, health, and safety. I was so glad that my past feelings of no one caring for me have proven to be wrong.

I used to take everything for granted. I guess it is fairly easy to forget the important things when so much seems wrong. I now know that when life throws me a curve, I can just get through it. I always used to ask "why?" about all the bad things, but I never asked "why not?" I know that the worst always turns into something a little better. When times are tough, I just got to keep a smile on my face and my chin up. I realize that every person has issues to deal with. I also just want to let you know that I really do like my new school and I am hoping to graduate from there someday. Not to sound rude, but I don't ever want to see you again!! In court, of course!

> **Sincerely,**
> **Ashley**

I have seen a lot of Ashleys—kids who turn away from their families and look to others to help them out. It often takes a while for them to see that those closest to them do care and that help is nearby. Ashley finally got tired of all the hassle—being on probation, getting caught for violating her terms, going back to court time after time, and then facing another stretch in jail. Luckily, she has the support of her family and the guidance of her probation officer. I don't want to sound rude either, but I don't ever want to see Ashley again—in court, of course.

FINAL THOUGHTS

Write down or discuss your thoughts:

- Are you surprised that Ashley went back to using drugs? Why or why not?
- Was there anything else the court could have tried to help Ashley? Or were all possible options used?
- Did you know that there is house arrest for teenagers? How would being under house arrest affect your behavior?
- Do you think Ashley's parents were right to take her and the marijuana to the police in the first place? Why or why not? If you began using drugs, would you want your parents to step in and "turn you in"?
- Have you ever felt unloved or unwanted by your parents? Did the feeling pass or does it still exist? Is it something you can discuss with them? Have you tried getting it out in the open? What would you like to say to them?

Did You Know?

- A 2002 survey of 1,000 students found that it was easier for students to get marijuana than cigarettes or beer, and 27 percent reported they could get marijuana in an hour or less.

• In 1999, 103,000 juveniles were arrested as runaways. About 60 percent were girls under 18 and 45 percent were under age 15.

• In 2003, a 6-year-old California boy brought to his 1st grade show-and-tell a small amount of marijuana, a pipe, and a lighter. He was suspended for five days and his father was arrested.

BRANDON, 14

breaking into a home

BRANDON'S BACKGROUND LEADING UP TO THE CRIME

Brandon is the youngest in his family. He has two older sisters and lives with his mother and step-father. His parents have been divorced for several years and each has remarried. Brandon has had little contact with his father since the divorce, but has a good relationship with his stepfather. His mother says there are no discipline problems at home, although she notices that he is quiet and moody sometimes as a result of the divorce.

Until recently, Brandon went to school regularly and played baseball. But toward the end of 8th grade he has some behavior problems and doesn't finish the school year. His mother pulls him out and plans to have him repeat the 8th grade in the fall.

Around this time, Brandon's friend takes a golf cart from a local course. The friend picks Brandon up and they drive it around until the battery dies. The boys leave the cart and go home. Brandon admits what he did and agrees to complete eight community service hours in the neighborhood. No formal charges are filed. He also takes a tour of a jail, accompanied by a corrections officer. This program is designed to prevent kids from getting in trouble. When Brandon finishes the community service, his case is closed.

BRANDON'S CRIME: BURGLARY

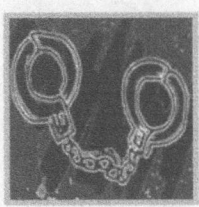

Brandon's friend, Colin, knows that a family will be gone from their home for the weekend. The two boys, both 13, go over to the house and climb in through a back window. They take jewelry from the home and run away. When the victims return, they discover the missing property and call the police. The investigation lasts seven months before Brandon and Colin are charged with the burglary. The stolen jewelry is recovered from the boys, who had hidden it, and is returned to the victims.

> ## Legal Definition of Burglary
>
> A person commits **BURGLARY** by entering or remaining unlawfully in or on a residential structure, a nonresidential structure, a fenced commercial or residential yard, with the intent to commit a theft or any felony therein.

YOUR CONCERNS AS A JUDGE

One year before the burglary, Brandon was involved in the incident with the stolen golf cart and did his eight hours of community service. You know that he's been having a difficult time with his parents' divorce and their new marriages. He's also been having trouble at school. He got family counseling when he was 12 and it appeared to make a difference. But then, at 13, Brandon is involved in the burglary. You need to determine if Brandon was the leader or just following his friend.

You are also concerned that in the seven-month period between the burglary and being charged, Brandon was involved in two other incidents.

In the first incident, Brandon lit a firecracker and threw it in the direction of three kids standing nearby. He admitted doing this, saying it was a joke and that he was not trying to hurt anyone. He told the police that it was a stupid thing to do and that he was sorry. He was charged with disorderly conduct.

About the same time, Brandon and another friend assaulted a boy at school. Brandon punched the victim in the face with his fist and an assault charge was filed against him.

Brandon appears before you on all of the charges. He pleads guilty to the assault and the burglary charge (reduced to criminal trespass as part of the plea bargain offered by the prosecutor—the agreement also called for dismissal of the disorderly conduct charge).

> See the definition of plea bargain in section entitled "Glossary of Legal and Court Terms Used in the Book".

Brandon's probation officer doesn't see him as a hardcore delinquent, but as a boy easily led by others into mischief. He recommends probation, attendance at a class on youth and the law, and some community service hours. Probation officers make recommendations to the judge, but you may accept, change, or reject the recommendations.

YOUR SENTENCING OPTIONS AS A JUDGE

Since Brandon had contact with the court the year before because of the stolen golf cart, you consider him a repeat or second offender. This means that the penalty has to be severe enough to keep him from returning to court a third time. Since burglary and assault are more serious than joyriding in a golf cart, the penalty needs to fit the crime. A home burglary usually carries at least probation if not some jail time, and payment to the victim for the items stolen. An assault charge usually results in some jail time, probation, and anger management classes.

Your options for Brandon's sentencing include:
- A jail sentence ranging from two weeks to a month, to get Brandon's attention, followed by one year of probation.
- A few hours or a weekend in jail, through a "Mock Lock-Up" program, followed by probation with services, including community service, anger management counseling, and a class on youth and the law.
- Probation for up to one year, with the threat of future jail time if Brandon messes up again.
- No probation, but some community service hours and payment to the burglary victim.
- Payment to the burglary victim and close the case.
- Anything else?

QUESTIONS TO CONSIDER BEFORE SENTENCING BRANDON

Write down or discuss your thoughts:
- The burglary and assault are Brandon's second and third offenses and more serious than his first. Is it time for Brandon to get a wake-up call? Does he need a taste of jail? Or is probation a better option? Why?
- How much weight do you give to the probation officer's report that Brandon is more of a follower than a leader? Does this influence what kind of sentence he gets? Why or why not?
- Brandon has problems in school and is repeating the 8th grade. Should anything be done to help him in school?

- Should more counseling be arranged to help Brandon deal with his feelings about the divorce and limited contact with his father? Is this any business of the court? Or is Brandon old enough to deal on his own with the good and the bad sides of divorce?
- In passing sentence, should a court take into account a young person's family life? If so, how? If not, why not?

YOU BE THE JUDGE

Complete this sentence:
Based on the information available to me, Brandon's sentence should be...

WHAT ACTUALLY HAPPENED

At his hearing, Brandon said he was sorry for the burglary and for getting into trouble again after being given another chance the year before. He wasn't surprised when I told him that he was being placed on probation. But he was surprised when we reviewed some of his probation terms.

- Our court had a new program designed for juveniles who had never been locked up, and I thought Brandon would fit right in. Called "Mock Lock-Up," it was just that—the young person spent three hours in jail. It was held during the day and Brandon would be with a corrections officer at all times. He was free to talk with the teens in jail and ask them questions. The program was meant to be a warning to kids tempted to commit crimes.
- I learned that Brandon had recently tried marijuana and alcohol. We talked about it and I wanted Brandon to see where he was headed if he didn't make some positive changes real soon. In addition to the "Mock Lock-Up" program, I ordered him to attend a one-day adult prison program. He

would have a chance to talk to adult inmates serving long sentences in prison, not just a few hours or days. Many of the inmates were there on drug-related charges, and most were between 18 and 25. I knew other juveniles who had attended this program. All reported that it scared them, shocked them, or left them speechless. The lessons stuck.

I also required Brandon to:
- Complete 30 hours of community service.
- Go to anger management classes, where he could deal with his feelings about his parents being divorced.
- Attend a class on youth and the law.

If all this didn't have an impact on Brandon, I might be out of options in getting my message across to him.

YOUR RESPONSE TO THE JUDGE'S DECISION

Write down or discuss your thoughts:
- Are you surprised by the judge's sentence? Why or why not?
- Was it harder or easier on Brandon than your sentence? In what ways?
- What part of the judge's sentence do you agree with? What part do you disagree with? Why?
- Is there anything important missing from Brandon's sentence? What is it and why is it important?
- What do you predict will happen to Brandon?

BRANDON AFTER SENTENCING

Brandon followed all of his probation terms and behaved well at home. He participated in the two "high impact" programs and said that he learned a lot that would help him in the future. He went to anger management classes and a class on youth and the law. He finished 30 hours of community service at a nearby park, picking up trash and washing the picnic tables and benches.

A few months before Brandon's 16th birthday, he was released from probation. Things went well for almost a year. Then he left home for a brief period and was cited for possession of alcohol. When he returned home, he got into a fight with his girlfriend and one of his sisters. Brandon was drunk at the time. He broke a door and hit both girls. When he threatened to get his BB gun, the police were called. Brandon was arrested and taken to jail. He stayed there for the next 20 days.

Letter from Brandon While He Was in Jail (age 16)

Your Honor,

This letter is to thank you very much for putting me in jail. It's not that I like this place. I never want to come back. You gave me 20 days to do a lot of thinking. During these 20 days, I've realized that I don't need drugs or my friends to complete my life. All I need is my family. I also realized that I don't want to be in jail five years from now. I would much rather have a successful job, along with my freedom, and my family. Thank you, your Honor.

Sincerely,
Brandon

Brandon admitted to one count of disorderly conduct by way of a plea bargain and the remaining charges were dismissed. At sentencing Brandon was put on intensive probation, given more community service hours, and ordered to visit adult prison again for the one-day program. He was 17 at the time, and I thought the "high impact" program might have more of an impact on him than when he was 14. In another year Brandon would be out of my control and eligible for adult jail, and I wanted him to see what was in store for him soon if he didn't change.

BRANDON TODAY

Brandon stayed out of trouble and his probation officer wrote a report recommending an early release. At 17, Brandon was once again released from the juvenile court's supervision. When last heard from, he was working at an auto service store and had stayed out of trouble.

It is rare that a judge receives a thank you note for locking someone up. The parents may thank you, depending on the circumstances, but seldom the juvenile. In this case, Brandon's letter seemed a sincere expression of a lesson learned. But actions speak louder than words, and the fact that Brandon stayed out of trouble shows that he meant what he said.

FINAL THOUGHTS

Write down or discuss your thoughts:
- Was Brandon's case handled the right way? Why or why not?
- Have you ever been tempted to go along with something that was illegal or wrong? What did you do? Looking back, would you do anything differently?
- What makes some kids leaders and others followers? Is it sometimes hard to take a stand and not go along with the crowd? What makes it tempting to join in an unlawful act, rather than passing it up?
- Isn't riding around in a golf cart or setting off a firecracker just a harmless prank? Aren't there much more serious crimes that should be

investigated and prosecuted? Should that type of teenage behavior be punished by the courts? Why or why not?
- Do you think "high impact" or "scared straight" programs (like having kids visit jails) stop kids from committing crime? Why or why not? Have you or someone you know ever participated in such a program? What impact, if any, did it have?
- Do you think Brandon will continue to stay out of trouble?

Did You Know?

- "Kids visit prison" programs started in the United States in the 1970s and have been tried in at least five other countries (Norway, Germany, Australia, Canada, and England). A 2001 report found them not effective unless combined with other services, such as probation and counseling (Petrosino, Turpin-Petrosino, and Buehler, Academy of Arts and Sciences and Harvard University, 2001: "The Effects of 'Scared Straight'

and Other Juvenile Awareness Programs on Subsequent Offending").
• In 2000 there were 10 deaths in the United States from fireworks with an estimated 11,000 persons treated for fireworks-related injuries. About 50 percent of those injured were age 14 and younger. Most of the injuries came from the use of firecrackers, bottle rockets, sparklers, cherry bombs, and M-80s (National Center for Injury Prevention and Control).

BRIANNE, 17

a stolen car, a stolen credit card, and forgery

BRIANNE'S BACKGROUND LEADING UP TO THE CRIME

Brianne lives with her parents and an older sister. She starts rebelling against her parents at a very young age. She first uses drugs while in grade school, and over the years she experiments with marijuana, crystal meth, alcohol, cocaine, and LSD.

When Brianne is 13, she gets into a fight with her father as they're driving home from the mall. It continues at home, with Brianne waving around a knife and kicking a hole in a wall. She is charged with disorderly conduct and criminal damage and is placed on probation. Shortly after, she runs away, violating her probation. Brianne returns to court several times for these and other probation violations (losing contact with her probation officer, not doing her community service hours, etc.). She keeps running away and going to jail.

Between ages 13 and 17, Brianne is charged with a variety of offenses, including possession of alcohol, DUI (driving under the influence of alcohol), false reporting (lying to a police officer), and disorderly conduct. Brianne admits the false reporting and the other charges are dismissed.

When Brianne comes before the court on the false reporting charge, she has one year left in the juvenile justice system before she turns 18. She has already been locked up on many occasions. She has also had two residential drug treatment placements, been hospitalized for depression, and received medication and drug counseling. But each time, she either ran away or was kicked out. Brianne is never in one place long enough for the programs to make a difference. The time has come to put Brianne where she can't run—where she can face her issues and work on them for a long time.

BRIANNE'S CRIMES: AUTO THEFT, CREDIT CARD THEFT, AND FORGERY

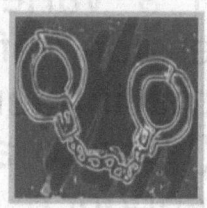

Shortly before Brianne can be locked up, she and her boyfriend approach a car and break the front window. Brianne finds car keys in a purse left on the front seat and they steal the car. They drive to a local dealership and use the victim's credit card to buy over $800 worth of car parts. Brianne signs the victim's name to the bill of sale. They abandon the car nearby. Three weeks later, Brianne and her boyfriend are arrested and charged with auto theft, credit card theft, and forgery. The prosecutor is asking that Brianne be sent to adult court on these charges.

Juvenile courts have control over children and teenagers until a designated age, depending on what state you live in. When a young person reaches the state's maximum age, the adult criminal system handles all new crimes, where the penalties, such as longer jail sentences or probation, are more severe. Some teens, depending on their age, criminal history, and current crime, can be tried and sentenced in adult court. The prosecutor can either file the charges in adult court or ask the juvenile court judge to send the juvenile to adult court on the charges. Each state has its own process to handle this type of case. The issue is how to best protect the community from the juvenile, and at the same time rehabilitate him or her in preparation for eventual release. A juvenile who is sent to adult jail is housed in separate quarters from the adult population.

Legal Definition of Auto Theft

A person commits **AUTO THEFT** if, without lawful authority, the person knowingly controls another person's means of transportation, with the intent to permanently deprive the person of such means of transportation, or does so knowing or having reason to know that the property is stolen.

Legal Definitions of Credit Card Theft and Forgery

A person commits **THEFT** if, without lawful authority, the person knowingly controls property of another, with the intent to deprive the other person of such property, or comes into control of lost, mislaid, or misdelivered property of another under circumstances providing means of inquiry as to the true owner, and appropriates such property to the person's own or another person's use, without reasonable efforts to notify the true owner.

A person commits **FORGERY** if, with the intent to defraud, the person

> falsely makes, completes, or alters a written instrument; or knowingly possesses a forged instrument; or offers or presents, whether accepted or not, a forged instrument or one that contains false information.

YOUR CONCERNS AS A JUDGE

You are well aware of Brianne's history, having met her in court dozens of times over the years. You think you have gotten to know her and her family fairly well, yet you don't know what is really behind Brianne's disruptive behavior. Whenever she comes to court she is very pleasant and, as her probation officer writes, "extremely easy to like." Both parents live with her. They seem caring and attend all her hearings.

You have a recent psychological report on Brianne, which states that there aren't any additional programs that could meet Brianne's needs. She has been through several hospitalizations, residential drug treatment programs, and group home placements without any success. She either ran away from each of these programs or was kicked out. Whenever she was back home, she acted out in an aggressive and self-destructive way. However, Brianne always does well when she's locked up in jail. She's committing serious crimes and abusing drugs and alcohol. What more can you do?

YOUR SENTENCING OPTIONS AS A JUDGE

Brianne is charged with three felonies—theft of the car and credit card, and forgery. You have the option of sending her to adult court on these charges, where she could get a longer sentence.

> A felony is a crime that may be punished by a year or more in jail or prison. A misdemeanor is a crime that may be punished by less than a year in jail or prison. Each state sets its own minimum and maximum jail sentences for specific crimes.
>
> Some states require that a juvenile with two felonies on her record be tried as an adult on the third felony charge. The third offense may be relatively minor, like shoplifting a $5 item, but with a prior history of felonies, the offender is still sent to adult court.

In Brianne's case there are two decisions to be made regarding the theft and forgery charges. First, should Brianne remain in juvenile court or be sent to adult court? If Brianne remains in juvenile court, she will be free from the system—including free from probation—when she turns 18. If she is tried as an adult, she may serve years in jail or on probation—well beyond her 18th birthday. Second, if sent to adult court, what would be an appropriate sentence considering her history?

Sentencing options available to you are:
- Send Brianne to adult court on these charges and let the adult court judge decide the penalty.
- Send Brianne to adult court with a recommendation for sentencing, since you know Brianne and her history. The recommendation is for adult probation for one to three years, with drug testing and counseling.
- Keep Brianne in juvenile court and send her to jail until she is 18, with drug counseling to prepare her for reentering society when she's released at that age.
- Anything else?

Letter from Brianne While in Jail Awaiting Sentencing (age 17)

Dear Judge Jacobs,

I am sure you are a very busy man, so just in case you have forgotten, I will tell you a little about myself. I have been in the system now for about five years. None of these times were for any major crimes, just basically runaway charges and drug problems. I was a stubborn kid. You have given me chance after chance after chance. And every time I have taken your time and patience for granted. You have spent thousands of dollars on me to try to give me the treatment I needed for my addiction to crystal meth, and every time I just turned around and proved to you that I was not a strong enough person to stay put and face my problems.

About two years ago I started injecting this horrible drug into my veins, which seemed to only bring me down ten times harder. And then, about five months ago, I was stopped while driving and arrested. I remained in jail for several weeks and was released.

I did take the time I was in jail to sober up and I managed to find the strength inside myself that everyone has been looking for all these years. I stayed away from the drugs. I kept in contact with my parents on a daily basis and rebuilt a relationship with them that I did not think was possible to do. I helped them out around the house, and for the first time since I was 12 years of age, I enjoyed living there and it actually felt like a family.

But I am afraid to say that I have picked up some new charges this time around, and I have to say they are somewhat serious crimes. Judge Jacobs, I am not writing you this letter to kiss your butt, or to lie to you and say that I didn't do the acts that I am accused of. For I am guilty of everything I am being charged with. But I do beg for your forgiveness and ask for just one more chance. One more chance to prove to you that I can get a job, get my GED, and maintain a normal life while living under my parents' roof.

Your honor, being with my parents made me realize that I want a normal life, an honest life, and most of all to have a place I can call home. Maybe it's just me growing up, but all I know is I want something for myself. I want to be somebody, not just another junkie on the streets. I have plans to be someone. Yes, I have committed a crime and I am prepared to take responsibility for what I've done. But please, before you decide what you are going to do to me, please keep in mind what I've said here, and also keep in mind that I went from sticking a needle in my arm daily to not doing drugs at all.

That is more strength in one little girl than any hero could have in a lifetime. And knowing I can do that, I know now I can do anything if I put my mind to it.

Sincerely,

Brianne

QUESTIONS TO CONSIDER BEFORE SENTENCING BRIANNE

Write down or discuss your thoughts:
- Can Brianne be helped by juvenile jail, in the remaining months before she turns 18? (Remember, once she turns 18, she won't be on probation if you keep her in the juvenile system.) Or should you send her to adult court, where she could get a longer sentence? Will adult jail shock Brianne into behaving responsibly?
- Brianne is only 17. Will adult jail do her more harm than good?
- What would make Brianne so rebellious and out-of-control at such

a young age? Her parents seem like nice people, but have no clue that Brianne has been doing drugs since grade school. Maybe something is happening at home to cause her to act out. Perhaps you can dig further to find the root of her problems. Should something have been done with Brianne's parents when she first came to court at 13? Should you do something now?
- Are some kids simply rebellious by nature, even if they've had a good home life? Does home life always explain a person's behavior? Does it ever justify a person's acts?
- Will Brianne's letter affect the sentence you give? Why or why not?

YOU BE THE JUDGE

Complete this sentence:

Based on the information available to me, Brianne's sentence should be...

WHAT ACTUALLY HAPPENED

Although Brianne had done well in the past in juvenile jail, I felt she needed the structure of probation or parole after her 18th birthday. The community would be protected from her in case she continued to commit crimes. The only way to accomplish that was for her to be tried as an adult on the theft and forgery charges. Brianne had not given me any reason to believe that she could become drug-free and law-abiding in the short time she could remain in the juvenile system.

Consequently, the new charges were forwarded to the adult court. I didn't make a recommendation on sentencing because I wasn't sure what programs would be available when she appeared in adult court. I also felt that the adult court would have her entire juvenile record and could decide what to do. Brianne would finish her five months in juvenile jail and then deal with the new charges before an adult criminal court judge.

YOUR RESPONSE TO THE JUDGE'S DECISION

Write down or discuss your thoughts:
- Are you surprised by the judge's sentence? Why or why not?
- Was it harder or easier on Brianne than your sentence? In what ways?
- What part of the judge's sentence do you agree with? What part do you disagree with? Why?
- Is there anything missing from Brianne's sentence? If so, what is it, and why is it important?
- How do you feel about the decision to refer Brianne to adult court even though she's 17? Do you think a longer adult sentence might have a

greater impact on her? Why or why not?
- What do you predict will happen to Brianne?

BRIANNE TODAY

Brianne got a break in adult court. Instead of jail time, she received three years probation as her sentence. As part of her probation, she had to submit to random drug tests.

Unfortunately, things didn't go well. Brianne was 18 when she was caught with marijuana and a pipe. Her probation was changed to a one-year sentence in adult prison. Brianne served her time in a women's facility, earned her GED while there, and was released.

Brianne is now a 21-year-old wife and mother of a baby boy. She continues to live with her parents, who baby-sit for her while she is at work. She is a sales clerk and is also attending cosmetology school in the evenings. She got married in order to be able to visit her husband, who was in jail.

Brianne has been drug-free for over a year. She also stopped smoking cigarettes when she became pregnant. After five years in the system, Brianne said she was sick of her past lifestyle. With a baby to care for, she wants "a normal life" without always looking over her shoulder. "Drugs destroy dreams," she stated, "but I wouldn't change anything, because it's what's made me what I am today."

Brianne was always afraid that she would lose someone close to her while she was in jail. Her worst fear came true when her best friend was killed in a car accident. They had been friends since they were 9. Because Brianne was in prison when the accident happened, she was not allowed to attend the funeral. She remembered her friend by getting a tattoo inscribed with a personal message.

During one of Brianne's times in jail, the school there sponsored a writing contest. Brianne entered several poems.

One of them was selected as a winner and was published.

Sunshine

I'm in way too deep now
I'm in way over my head
Consequences lying ahead of me
Are something that I dread

I've seen the lowest of low
And been the highest of high
But when it's all over
Something inside you dies

I could be a coward
Lower my head and cry
Crawl into my cell
Then lie down and die

But I know life's not over
My heart tells me to fight
And if I look hard enough
I see my freedom in sight

Though I am behind these bars
I'll start my life anew
Despite these walls around me
My sun will still shine through

FINAL THOUGHTS

Write down or discuss your thoughts:
- Were you surprised that Brianne started doing drugs again? Were you surprised that she stopped? Do you think she'll stay off drugs?
- Should juveniles be treated like adults in some cases (tried in adult court and sent to adult jail)? In what kinds of cases?
- Have you ever felt like Brianne, that your life is out of control? It doesn't have to involve drugs—it could be stress about work or school, or conflicts in your family. What causes you stress? What could you do to reduce stress in your life?
- When you've tried to be independent in your life, what has been the response from your parents? Are you able to tell them

how you feel and reach an understanding? Why or why not?
- Have your parents been there for you when you've gotten into trouble? Would you stick by your son or daughter if they made a mistake?

Did You Know?

In 2000, there were 21,130 juveniles being held in adult facilities nationwide (Children's Defense Fund 2002, Office of Juvenile Justice and Delinquency Prevention 2000).

CARLA, 15

a fight with mom

CARLA'S BACKGROUND LEADING UP TO THE CRIME

Carla lives with her mother, two brothers, and a sister. Little is known about her father, including where he currently lives. The family is poor and they don't have a car. Carla starts working when she's 15 to help out. She gets a job through a community teen program and works part-time as a secretary.

Carla usually has trouble getting up in the morning, and her mother sometimes tries to wake her by yelling at her or throwing a glass of water on her. During one of these wake-up calls, Carla gets upset and starts yelling and screaming at her mother. She throws cans and part of a bedpost at her mother and yanks the phone out of the wall, damaging the cord and wall plug. The police are called and Carla is charged with disorderly conduct and criminal damage.

Since this is her first offense, she's permitted to remain at home until sentencing if she participates in counseling. Carla agrees and the situation at home calms down. Her sentencing will take place in 30 days.

CARLA'S CRIME: AGGRAVATED ASSAULT

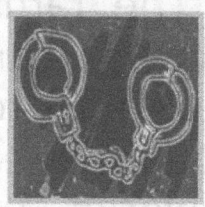

While at home waiting for sentencing, Carla gets into another fight with her mother. She is asleep again and her mother throws a glass of water in her face. Carla becomes angry, grabs a pair of scissors, and threatens to kill her mother. She stabs a nearby dresser three times. Her mother wrestles the scissors away from her and calls the police. Carla, 16, is arrested and taken to jail. She denies having the scissors at any time during the argument.

Legal Definition of Aggravated Assault

A person commits **AGGRAVATED ASSAULT** by intentionally, knowingly, or recklessly causing physical injury to another person; by using a deadly weapon or dangerous instrument in the course of assaulting another; or if the assault victim is a peace officer, teacher, paramedic, firefighter, or probation officer.

YOUR CONCERNS AS A JUDGE

After meeting Carla in court and talking with her mother, it's clear to you that a cooling off period is needed. Carla, like most kids, wants more independence and thinks her mother is always on her about something. She does realize, however, that her short fuse contributes to problems at home.

But you also have concerns about her mother's behavior and parenting techniques. Her mother wants Carla to follow the rules and learn to control her temper, but is throwing water in someone's face really the best way to wake her up? Maybe you can give some suggestions or offer training that may help resolve some of their issues.

The juvenile court's psychologist sees Carla during her time in jail and reports no medical or mental health problems. The doctor describes Carla as a cooperative, pleasant young lady, who appears to have reasonable insight into her own behavior. Carla sees herself as a positive person with good self-esteem. She wants to finish school and become a nurse. Her goals are realistic and within her reach. She understands that there are alternatives to her anger, such as taking a time out or a walk. Carla has admitted using marijuana in the past and is willing to take random drug tests to show that she is staying away from drugs.

You also know that Carla's mother went through the court system when she was a youth and was locked up for a period of time. She does not want Carla to be in the same situation and is trying to give her a loving home. She wants Carla to be successful and is willing to take her back.

You have to decide whether it is safe for Carla to return to her family. Sentencing is soon and she's been in jail for two months. She has received counseling while there and has learned a lot about herself. But is it enough to guarantee that next time Carla loses her temper she won't cause serious harm to someone? Will she use a knife instead of scissors the next time? Are her promises and good behavior in jail enough to risk letting her go home? And if so, under what terms? Would you require anything of her mother? What safety net can you put in place to keep the peace at home?

> Carla spent two months in jail before sentencing, waiting to be evaluated and for her report to be written for the court. Due to the large number of cases in juvenile court and a limited number of judges to hear them, long periods in jail before sentencing are common.

YOUR SENTENCING OPTIONS AS A JUDGE

The sentencing options available in juvenile court for assault are fairly broad. The young person's history and family life are usually taken into consideration in deciding the right penalty. In Carla's favor is the fact that no one was injured in either incident and she was provoked by her mother. Not in Carla's favor is that there was a previous fight with the mother and Carla denied using the scissors in the most recent incident. In a case such as Carla's, you suspect that her behavior at home is just the tip of the iceberg—that there is a lot below the surface that needs to be explored. Simply telling her to shape up or giving her a few community service hours is not the answer.

Your options include:
- Keep Carla in jail for an additional month until further evaluations are done, including a psychiatric evaluation for medication purposes and a recommendation for additional treatment, if necessary.
- A jail sentence of between two to three months, with intensive counseling while in jail, with probation for up to one year after release.
- Place Carla in foster care while you do more research on what the family needs.
- Placement in a residential drug treatment facility for six months before returning home, and counseling for Carla's mother to

prepare her for her daughter's return.
- Probation for one year, along with family counseling and drug testing.
- Anything else?

QUESTIONS TO CONSIDER BEFORE SENTENCING CARLA

Write down or discuss your thoughts:
- Carla has already spent 60 days in jail awaiting sentencing. Should she be punished any more? Is there anything to gain from sentencing her to more jail time?
- What do you think of the parenting skills of Carla's mother? How much is Carla's mother to blame for her daughter's behavior? What can you do about this?

- Should counseling be provided for all family members or just to Carla? How do you get to the bottom of what triggers Carla's conflicts with her mother?
- Are you worried that Carla's behavior at home affects her brothers and sister? Should you find out whether they want her home or are afraid of her? How much should the reaction of the brothers and sister affect your decision?
- If Carla goes home, what precautions can you take to prevent fights and protect her family members?

YOU BE THE JUDGE

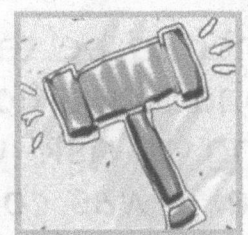

Complete this sentence:
 Based on the information available to me, Carla's sentence should be...

WHAT ACTUALLY HAPPENED

It was fortunate that Carla's mother, brothers, and sister came to her sentencing. I was able to see them interact and discuss with them my concerns about letting Carla return home. They said they weren't afraid of Carla coming home. She had behaved herself in jail during the past two months, and now it was time to see if she could maintain the same attitude at home.

- I released her from jail and placed her on probation for one year.
- I ordered that the entire family work with a therapist who would come into the home several times a week.
- I ordered her to be tested for drugs by her probation officer.

I was taking a risk with whatever decision I made. I was concerned about letting Carla go home because I wasn't sure she'd be able to control her temper. On the other hand, she hadn't lost her temper while in jail and I saw little to gain by keeping her locked up. The time had come to see if Carla learned anything from jail and the counseling she received while there.

YOUR RESPONSE TO THE JUDGE'S DECISION

Write down or discuss your thoughts:
- Are you surprised by the judge's sentence? Why or why not?
- Was it harder or easier on Carla than your sentence? In what ways?
- What part of the judge's sentence do you agree with? What part do you disagree with? Why?
- Is there something missing from Carla's sentence? If so, what is it and why is it important?
- What do you predict will happen when Carla returns home?

CARLA AFTER SENTENCING

At first Carla stayed out of trouble, doing everything her mother and probation officer expected. But after several months, one of her drug tests came back positive for cocaine. Carla was charged with possession of narcotics and violating her probation (she didn't contact her probation officer as required). Once again, Carla was locked up, this time for 28 days.

Letter from Carla While in Jail (age 16)

Dear Judge Jacobs,

I really enjoy living at home with my family and siblings and really miss them now. I messed up sir, not my mom, so please, it is not my mom's fault. It's my fault that I'm back in here, hopefully for the last time. I'm afraid that this is my last chance to change before I end up in jail. If you ask me if I deserve to go there, I would say no because I'm not a bad person at all. But we all make mistakes in life.

To tell you the truth, I really enjoy going to school and work. I would like to say I have been doing nothing but positive things in here.

So please, can you give me another chance? I've been in here two times and that's enough for me to learn my lesson. I pray to God to be released back to my mother.

These are the positive things I have been doing (and I was only ordered to do three positive things but I did a lot more):

Positive things I have done:

1) Going to school and got a total of 10 credits.

2) Going to church on Tuesday and Sunday.

3) Completed a drug treatment program and received my diploma.

4) Studying for my G.E.D.

5) Received my red shirt and still got my shirt.

> *I have a plan for when I get out, and that is to join the Job Corps. That will help me stay out of trouble and away from my old friends. I can live at home with my family and spend more time with them. Right now, I really miss my mom and little brother and sister, even my older brother. Every night I cry because I have messed up. I pray for those mothers out there like my mom—a single parent working hard to keep food on the table and a roof over our heads and clothes on four kids' backs. Thank god for my mom and older brother being there at a time like this, and most of all for keeping us together. May I please have another chance with my family and at life out there in the world?*
>
> *Sincerely,*
> *Carla*

After Carla was released from jail, she was placed in foster care because her mother refused to have her at home until the family could move to a better neighborhood, where there were less drugs and crime. Carla settled down while in foster care and after a few months returned to her mother. She remained on probation until she was 17, when she was successfully released from the juvenile court's supervision.

> When a juvenile goes to jail, points are given for good behavior. If the juvenile obeys the rules she gains privileges, such as a later bedtime or participation in gym. Inmates wear shirts of different colors, depending on the level they've reached. They start at the lowest level, wearing a white shirt, and can advance to a blue shirt, then yellow, then red, the highest level. A violation means a loss of points and a return to the lower color shirt. When the inmate returns to court for her hearing, the judge takes shirt color into consideration in deciding whether to release the juvenile or what kind of sentence to give.

CARLA TODAY

Carla is now 20. She has two sons and continues to live with her mother. When I talked to her recently, she said, "After a total of three months in jail, I decided to change. I didn't want to be locked up for two years, until I turned 18. My mom moved us away from my old friends. I don't know where I'd be if my mom didn't lock me up—probably doing drugs or maybe dead."

Carla worked for a fast-food chain for three years and became a manager. She left that position to earn more money and is now a cashier for a major hotel chain. She has a clean record as an adult and is still interested in becoming a nurse. She enjoys going to the park with her family and playing basketball.

FINAL THOUGHTS

Write down or discuss your thoughts:
- What is your reaction to the letter Carla wrote from jail?
- Carla had a hard time growing up in a neighborhood with crime and drugs. How has your neighborhood affected you? What would you most like to change about your neighborhood?
- Were you surprised to read that Carla has two children? Were you surprised to read that she is taking care of them?
- Do you or does someone close to you have a short temper? Do you know what your hot buttons are and how to control them? Is your safety or the safety of other family members at risk? Is there someone you can go to for help or advice?

Did You Know?

A national survey showed that girls ages 9–14 are as violent as boys:

- 66 percent said they had seen 1–10 fights during the past year; 10 percent had witnessed more than 10 fights.
- 36 percent had been in physical fights during the past year; 33 percent fought another girl, 30 percent fought a boy.
- 72 percent had "seen or heard" of girls who carry weapons; 17 percent carried weapons themselves.

The girls gave these reasons for being violent:

- they've been victims of violence themselves (54 percent)
- they want to look tough (50 percent)
- they don't have a good family life (43 percent)
- they want to get even with someone (41 percent)
- they need to protect themselves (38 percent)

(Center for Women Policy Studies, Washington, D.C.)

CHARLES, 16

cocaine and a gun

CHARLES'S BACKGROUND LEADING UP TO THE CRIME

Charles lives with his grandmother, who is also his legal guardian. She is in her 70s and does her best to help Charles stay out of trouble. An aunt also lives in the home and is additional support for Charles. His parents are not married and live in other states. Charles receives an occasional telephone call from his mother and has no contact with his father. Two older siblings live away from home and have little contact with Charles.

Charles first gets into trouble at age 11. He and a dozen other kids assault a boy in an attempt to jump him (initiate him) into a gang. Charles admits hitting the boy, but denies he belongs to the gang. The matter is adjusted and no formal charges are filed. Charles completes seven hours of counseling as a consequence (penalty).

> In many cases, a prosecutor may decide to handle a crime without filing a formal charge. If the juvenile admits what he or she did, the matter is "adjusted." The prosecutor decides the penalty and the case stays out of court. The advantage is that the juvenile does not have a record, which would have an affect in school and on job applications. Also, in some jurisdictions the word "consequence" is the same as "penalty."

The following year, at age 12, Charles is cited for violating curfew. Except for a few truancy and curfew violations, Charles stays out of trouble until age 16.

CHARLES'S CRIME: POSSESSION OF

NARCOTICS AND MISCONDUCT WITH WEAPONS

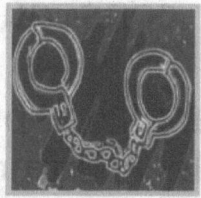

Charles is seen by the police on the street after midnight, hanging around the passenger side of a car. He looks down at the ground and then at the police. Because of the time of night, they approach Charles and ask him how old he is. The police tell him to stay put because it's after curfew.

The officers find a plastic bag containing a rock-like substance in the area where Charles is standing. He blurts out that it doesn't belong to him. Then, while being placed in the police car, Charles admits that the baggie is his but that he doesn't sell drugs. He explains that his mother gave him money for new shoes, and that just before the police arrived, he used the money to buy the drugs. Charles says that the drugs are for his personal use only, and that he has been smoking crack cocaine for the past year.

Before he is handcuffed and put in the police car, Charles is searched and a loaded gun is found in his pocket. He tells the police that he bought the gun earlier that night for $20 from an unknown male. Charles is taken into custody and is charged with drug possession and carrying a concealed weapon.

Legal Definitions of Possession of Narcotic Drugs and Misconduct with Weapons

A person shall not knowingly possess, use, sell, transport or manufacture any nonprescription **DRUG,** or any other drug listed in the state's controlled substances statute.

A person commits **MISCONDUCT WITH WEAPONS** by knowingly carrying a deadly weapon without a permit, except a pocket knife; possessing a deadly weapon if such person is a prohibited possessor; carrying a deadly weapon in a public

> place after a reasonable request by the operator of the place to remove the weapon; or by possessing such on school grounds.

YOUR CONCERNS AS A JUDGE

You are surprised when you first meet Charles, who comes to court with his grandmother and aunt. You reviewed his file before the hearing and are aware of his alleged gang involvement. However, the young person who stands before you is a well-groomed, confident individual, unlike the gang members you're used to seeing. Charles's record does not match the person in front of you.

This case would be easier to decide if Charles was a runaway or didn't have a family. In that case, because of the seriousness of his crimes, sending Charles to jail would be the easiest and most obvious thing to do. However, Charles has a family who cares about him, although they apparently don't know everything he's up to.

Drugs and weapons are a dangerous combination. At sentencing Charles will be 17 with eleven months left in the juvenile system. The issue facing you as a judge is how to best use this time to balance what is best for Charles with the community's right to protection.

YOUR SENTENCING OPTIONS AS A JUDGE

When a juvenile is caught with drugs, probation and a drug treatment program are the usual options. If the quantity of drugs is large and selling is suspected, the crime is more serious. In Charles's case, he denied selling and said it was for his personal use. Based on the quantity involved, his claim was believable. But add to this incident possession of a loaded gun and the seriousness of the situation increases. An adult in Charles's position would be facing several years of jail time, followed by several years of probation. Although only 16, Charles is a serious offender requiring a strong message. Your sentencing options include, but are not limited to:

- An 11-month jail sentence, until Charles is 18.
- Intensive (daily) probation with the threat of deferred jail time if Charles gets in more trouble later on, along with a drug treatment program, an order to find a job, and a ban on possessing weapons.
- Regular probation, with a gun safety class, and community service hours.
- Anything else?

> A judge may order time in jail to be served at a future date, or "deferred." If the juvenile behaves, the time may be suspended and never served.

> Intensive probation means daily supervision by a probation officer either by telephone or personal visits—sometimes twice a day. It generally lasts 6 to 12 months.

QUESTIONS TO CONSIDER BEFORE SENTENCING CHARLES

Write down or discuss your thoughts:
- Should Charles be locked up for the next 11 months, until he's 18? Would that give him the best chance to succeed as an adult, since he would at least be away from drugs and may benefit from some of the department's programs? Or would nearly a year of jail possibly harden Charles and turn him into an adult criminal

when he gets out? Since there are no guarantees either way, which way do you go?
- Are you worried more about the drug charge, the gun charge, or both equally? Why?
- Are you worried about the alleged gang involvement? What can you do about it?
- How much weight do you give to his lack of family support? Although he lives with his grandmother and aunt, they don't really have much control over him. Charles may be polite when he's home, but the problem is that he's never there. If he comes and goes as he pleases, how is the community protected from his activities? Would you order parenting classes for his grandmother and aunt, or is it too late? What else?
- Would you inquire further about his mother and father—why they live out-of-state and don't help raise their son? Do you think Charles would change his ways if allowed to move to his mother's or father's home? Would anything be different?

Aren't drugs and guns available everywhere?

YOU BE THE JUDGE

Complete this sentence:
Based on the information available to me, Charles's sentence should be...

WHAT ACTUALLY HAPPENED

By the time we were back in court, Charles had served 41 days in jail awaiting sentencing. There were no discipline problems while he was there. I decided to release him to his grandmother on intensive probation. I explained to Charles that he would have not only a regular probation officer, but also a surveillance officer who would keep track of him on a daily basis.

As part of his probation I ordered him to:

- Participate in a drug treatment program.
- Return to school or find a job.
- Not possess any type of weapon, including guns, knives, and hunting equipment.

I told Charles that this was his last chance. If there were any probation violations or new charges, he would be locked up until he turned 18.

YOUR RESPONSE TO THE JUDGE'S DECISION

Write down or discuss your thoughts:
- Are you surprised by the judge's sentence? Why or why not?
- Was it harder or easier on Charles than your sentence? In what ways?
- What part of the judge's sentence do you agree with? What part do you disagree with? Why?

- Is there anything missing from the judge's sentence that might have helped Charles and his family? If so, what is it? If not, why not?
- Do you think Charles will stay off drugs and keep out of trouble?

CHARLES AFTER SENTENCING

Even on intensive probation, Charles had trouble staying home and away from drugs. His whereabouts weren't always known and warrants were issued for his arrest. At one point, Charles left the state to live with his mother. To his credit, he voluntarily returned when he was told that there was a warrant out for him. After three months on intensive probation he was arrested again, this time for possession of marijuana. This was his fourth trip to jail. Six months remained before Charles turned 18. He expected to remain locked up until his 18th birthday. While in jail, Charles wrote me the following letter, asking for leniency.

Letter from Charles While in Jail (age 17)

Dear Judge Jacobs:
I'm writing you to ask if you can see that I get paroled early. I honestly am putting the drugs and negative people behind me. My girlfriend had the baby and I cried like a baby. I missed a very important time in my life. Why? Because I chose to use drugs. I chose to make bad choices that would affect my daughter's first six months of life. I am not ever, I mean never, gonna use another drug or associate with bad people. Even if you don't give me another chance, I'll surround myself with positive people. I honestly never will do anything to get me separated from my family. I'm putting my grandma through so much stress, it's not good for her. She just reached her 82nd birthday. I don't want to be in jail if (I hate to say it) my grandma passes. I am a changed person, I just want to hold my job,

> ***complete my GED, and start college.***
> 　　***Sincerely,***
> 　　***Charles***

As I told Charles before, I had no choice but to stick to my word. Despite his pleas, I could not release him early. Charles remained locked up until his 18th birthday. He was then released to his grandmother.

CHARLES TODAY

It wasn't long before Charles returned to the streets and the drug scene. He was an adult when he was caught again with drugs and was sentenced to a five-year prison term. Charles is now 22 and nearing the end of his sentence. While in prison, Charles has taken some college courses and he plays the drums in a heavy-metal prison band. He plans to stay clean so that he can have a relationship with his daughter. Charles has always talked about his baby and her mother. I hope that, once he is free again, he will let his child be the focus of a drug-free, successful life.

Letter from Charles While in Adult Prison

Dear Judge Jacobs:

Thank you for responding to my letter. Once I read the letter you sent me, that I wrote to you a few years back, it took me on a, should I say, mental reminiscing trip. I compared that letter to the mistakes I made, which led to my being in jail now. I still believe that I have a chance to live comfortably—me and my daughter—without getting involved in the sales of narcotics. However, I am fully aware that my chances of success and my resources are extremely limited because of my felony conviction.

Sincerely,
Charles

In another letter Charles wrote me, he talked about losing his freedom: "I've learned to take nothing for granted. I've learned to take responsibility for my actions. I've noticed the changes in my body from being without drugs." His goals "are to provide a decent life for my daughter. Remain drug-free, and go into business running my own lawn service. Try to live like a normal person."

FINAL THOUGHTS

Write down or discuss your thoughts:
- Did the fact that Charles returned to drugs surprise you? Why or why not?
- Could anything else have been done to change the outcome? Why or why not?
- Do you know someone like Charles—who loves his family, but is determined to do whatever he

likes regardless of the law? Why do you think some teens act this way?
- Have you ever intentionally done something wrong to get attention—even if it's negative attention? What happened in your situation? Were you able to turn the negative into a positive? Why or why not?
- How do you think Charles's family influenced his behavior? How does your family situation affect the way you act?
- What do you think will happen to Charles in the future? Why?

Did You Know?

- In 1996, 25 percent of students ages 9–12 report that they have been offered, sold, or given an illegal drug at school in the last year (Partnership for a Drug Free America).
- In 1999, 7 percent of 12-to 17-year-olds used marijuana, while 7 percent used cocaine, 19 percent used alcohol, and 16 percent used tobacco.
- In 2000, 37,600 juveniles were arrested for possessing or carrying

weapons. 10 percent of those arrested were girls, and 33 percent were under age 15 (Office of Juvenile Justice and Delinquency Prevention Statistical Briefing Book 2002).

- By the late 1990s, every state, including 2,500 cities and the District of Columbia, reported youth gang problems. The states with the largest number of gang cities were California, New Jersey, Illinois, Texas, and Florida. Responsible for the growth of gangs are drugs, fatherless families, immigration, and media response (OJJDP 2001).

- In 1999, 17 percent of students reported the presence of gangs in their schools. Weapons on campus are reported more often at these schools than those without a gang presence (Children's Defense Fund 2001 Yearbook).

ERICA, 14

assault and possessing a marijuana pipe

ERICA'S BACKGROUND LEADING UP TO THE CRIME

Erica lives with her parents and two older brothers. The family is very poor and Erica is having problems in school. At age 12, she starts cutting classes with one excuse or another. She finally tells her mother that she is not getting along with some of the girls at school.

When Erica is 13, her family's home burns down. They also have car problems and her father's health isn't good. A few months later, in the 7th grade, Erica is raped. She becomes pregnant and, with the advice and counseling of her parents, decides to have an abortion.

ERICA'S CRIME: ASSAULT AND POSSESSION OF DRUG PARAPHERNALIA

Erica joins a few friends for a sleepover at her friend's home. Some of Erica's money turns up missing and she confronts the suspected thief at school a few days later. When the girl denies stealing the money, Erica slams the girl's head down on a table and punches her in the face and stomach. Erica is charged with assault and admits the crime in court.

While waiting for sentencing on the assault charge, Erica and another girl are seen passing marijuana back and forth during a test in school. She is sent to the office and the assistant principal asks Erica what happened.

Erica denies having anything illegal. Her backpack is searched and a black pipe containing marijuana is found. The police are called and question Erica. She admits that the pipe is hers and that she uses it to smoke marijuana. Erica is charged with possession of drug paraphernalia (the pipe), admits to attempted possession, and is released on house arrest to await sentencing.

Legal Definitions of Assault and Possession of Drug Paraphernalia

A person commits **ASSAULT** by intentionally, knowingly, or recklessly causing any physical injury to another person, intentionally placing another person in reasonable fear of being injured, or knowingly touching another person with the intent to injure, insult, or provoke such person.

It is unlawful for any person to use or **POSSESS** with the intent to use **DRUG PARAPHERNALIA,** which means all equipment, products, and materials of any kind which are used, intended for use, or designed for use in injecting, ingesting, or inhaling any drug that is prohibited by law, including scales; spoons; capsules; balloons; syringes; needles; water pipes; metal, wooden, glass or ceramic pipes; roach clips; and bongs.

YOUR CONCERNS AS A JUDGE

You have not seen a young girl with so many problems in a long time. There is no question that Erica has had a very difficult childhood. Any one of her experiences would be terribly painful for an adult, but for one 14-year-old to suffer through so much is truly sad. She has admitted to turning to drugs to deal with life and "take the pain away."

Even though personal and family problems are no excuse for breaking the law, they also cannot be ignored.

Erica's behavior was obviously a result of her living situation and personal problems. How do you find a balance between helping Erica and holding her responsible for her actions? Is one more important than the other? Recognizing that you have many other cases, and that time and money are limited, what is the single most important thing you can do for Erica?

YOUR SENTENCING OPTIONS AS A JUDGE

Normally an assault of this type would result in a penalty that matched the injuries suffered by the victim. Payment for any medical bills would also be required. The marijuana pipe in Erica's backpack is another signal of trouble that you can't ignore. Probation is a sure thing, but what else could be done to help her? Your options are:

- Jail time ranging from a week to a month, depending on Erica's behavior during house arrest and her attitude in court, with probation for up to one year afterwards.
- Intensive probation, with individual and family counseling.
- Regular probation, with participation in an intensive four-day drug treatment program, along with drug testing and individual and family counseling.
- No probation, but anger management classes and ongoing counseling, including therapy for the rape.
- Placement in a residential treatment facility, a group home where the kids have counseling, peer groups, etc.
- Community service.
- Payment to the victim, if asked for.
- Anything else?

QUESTIONS TO CONSIDER BEFORE SENTENCING ERICA

Write down or discuss your thoughts:
- You may be asking yourself where to begin with Erica. Would more information about Erica's past help you to decide what do to? If so, what information would you like to have? If not, why is the information you have already enough?
- Family problems are a big factor in Erica's life. Can any court look at a crime without looking at the family issues that might influence the person's actions? How much do you take Erica's family situation into account in deciding what to do?
- Erica is evaluated by a psychologist and is found to be depressed and becoming more withdrawn. It's not

surprising that she was trying to escape the pain in her life through drugs. How would you address Erica's depression and drug abuse? (A lot of this depends on what programs for teens are available in your community and how much they cost. You can't ignore the fact that Erica's family is unable to pay for counseling or drug treatment.)

- Erica was raped at age 13, resulting in a pregnancy and then an abortion. Would you require Erica to go to rape counseling, even if you knew she didn't want to talk about the incident?
- Would you consider removing Erica from her home and placing her in a residential treatment facility (like a group home)? Or, if her family was cooperative, would you keep her at home but provide intensive services for all family members? (For example, arrangements can be made for individual and family counseling in the home three or four times a week. Also, her probation officer can have daily

contact with Erica in person or by phone.)
- Does Erica simply need some jail time to "get her attention"? Or would jail make things worse in this situation?
- Knowing Erica's history, what would you say to her parents at sentencing?

YOU BE THE JUDGE

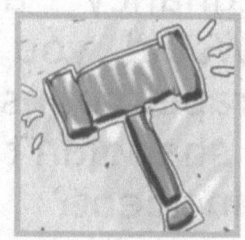

Complete this sentence:
Based on the information available to me, Erica's sentence should be...

WHAT ACTUALLY HAPPENED

Erica and her parents attended the hearing. The victim of the assault and her mother also came to court. Erica apologized to the girl for her conduct and said it wouldn't happen again. Her apology was accepted, and since there were no injuries, there were no medical bills Erica had to pay.

It was a good sign when Erica turned around in court to face her victim and apologize. She was sincere and seemed to want to put all of this behind her. We talked about her past and the need to look at it as just that—history. Erica said that her future was hers to make and that she wanted to do better. I was willing to see if she could remain at home and out of trouble. I placed her on probation for the next year, with special terms that she needed to follow:

- Our court had an intensive four-day drug counseling program for girls, which was conducted overnight in jail. I sentenced Erica to attend the program, during which she would participate in classroom instruction, role playing, a question and answer period, open discussion and debate, and one-on-one interviews with professional staff.
- She had to be tested for drug use.
- She was required to participate in individual and family counseling.

- She had to attend school every day.

The combination of jail and drug education seemed appropriate for Erica. I told her that I would check on her progress in the class, and did not want to see her in court again for any reason. Erica promised to do her best, as did her parents.

But what actually happens in the real world is often different from what people say in court. I hoped that Erica would really follow through on her promises.

YOUR RESPONSE TO THE JUDGE'S DECISION

Write down or discuss your thoughts:
- Are you surprised by the judge's sentence? Why or why not?
- Was it harder or easier on Erica than your sentence? In what ways?

- What part of the judge's sentence do you agree with? What part do you disagree with? Why?
- What's missing from the judge's decision? Is there something that Erica or her family needs, that wasn't in the judge's decision? What is it?

ERICA AFTER SENTENCING

For almost six months, Erica did well at home. She and her family participated in weekly counseling and it seemed to be helpful. Although they were still poor, Erica's family was getting by. Then her old habits returned. She stopped going to school and was caught again with a marijuana pipe. She admitted to possession of the pipe and was kept on probation. Everything calmed down again for a short period, until Erica ran away from home for a few weeks. When she returned, I now had to consider other options since she had violated her probation. She was locked up for two weeks waiting for her sentencing. During this period she wrote me the following letter.

Erica's Letter from Jail (age 14)

To Judge Jacobs,

I'm writing you this letter not for you to feel sorry for me, but to let you know the reasons for my misbehavior. A lot of things have happened to me over the past three years. It's more than I could handle at the time. So I went about everything the wrong way.

Maybe I could have went to my mom for help, but I knew she had her own problems to deal with. At the time, it seemed like everyone in my family did. I really had nowhere else to turn. So I turned to the wrong things.

I swear, if I could, I would take all of it back, but what is done can't be changed. So I'm just going to have to make the best of it now. We just moved into our dream house. It might not be much to others, but to us it's like the best thing in the world.

I will be going to a new school. That way I can meet new friends and just start all over again. I'm going to be getting all the help I need. I'm also going to be put on medication, so that will help a lot.

I'm willing to accept the consequences you have given me. I have been trying to stay out of trouble. Hopefully this will be the last time I come to court for something bad.
Sincerely,
Erica

Erica said she would try not to run away again, but couldn't promise me anything. With that comment, I felt that sending her home was not the answer. It was time to try a residential treatment facility or group home, where she would live away from home and get services. If she was in a secure setting where she couldn't run, maybe she would concentrate on the programs available to help her.

ERICA TODAY

As it turned out, Erica did well and was released from the program after six months. Her mother reported that everything at home was going well and that Erica planned on returning to school.

Just before school was to start, Erica, now 16, lost contact with her probation officer and stopped her drug testing. She ran away from home and a warrant for her arrest was issued. Her current whereabouts remain unknown.

FINAL THOUGHTS

Write down or discuss your thoughts:
- Are you surprised about what happened to Erica? Why or why not?
- Do you feel that everything possible was done to help Erica?
- If Erica is found and ends up back before the court, what would you do next? What could the court try that it hasn't yet tried?
- Do you know anyone who has been sexually assaulted or the victim of rape? Did that person get any help dealing with the incident? How did the incident affect her?
- Do you know the signs of depression? Could you recognize if a friend was suffering from depression? What would you say or do to help that person?
- Have family or personal problems ever made you so depressed that you felt out of control? Did anyone understand what you were going through? Were you able to get help for your depression?
- What will Erica need to do in the future to get her life back on track?

Did You Know?

• In 1999, 103,000 juveniles were arrested as runaways. About 60 percent were girls under 18 and 45 percent were under age 15. Over 500,000 children each year are "thrown away," told to leave home, abandoned, or not claimed when picked up as runaways (Juvenile Offenders and Victims: A National Report, National Center for Juvenile Justice).

• Rape statistics from the latest reporting year (2000) show that 4,500 juveniles were arrested for forcible rape. Ninety-nine percent of those arrested were boys and 39 percent were under age 15 (Office of Juvenile Justice and Delinquency Prevention Statistical Briefing Book 2002).

JENNIFER, 13

stolen Christmas presents

JENNIFER'S BACKGROUND LEADING UP TO THE CRIME

Jennifer has two brothers and a sister. She primarily lives with her mother, since her parents divorced when she was 3. Her father lives in another state.

The family moves from place to place as Jennifer's mother struggles to pay the bills. At one point the family loses both their rented house and their car. Jennifer's mother has to take the bus everywhere while they live in a motel. Jennifer starts working at age 10 to help out the family. She works at a hair salon after school and on weekends, setting up appointments for customers. Sometimes, though, she has to miss school for work.

Jennifer does well when she goes to school. She reads above her grade level and participates in sports, playing football and soccer. She joins the band and plays both the clarinet and violin.

But she also experiments with drugs throughout her childhood. She starts taking sips of alcohol from her mother's drinks at age 8. By age 12 she has tried marijuana, crack, speed, and ecstasy, and runs away from home whenever she feels like it.

Jennifer has her first contact with the law at age 12. She and three girlfriends enter a Wal-Mart store and go to the jewelry section. Jennifer takes two necklaces and an ear cuff. She then goes into the restroom and puts the jewelry in her pants pocket. One friend, a 13-year-old, puts the jewelry she took into her purse. The two other girls don't take anything.

The girls leave the restroom and together walk past the cash registers and out of the store. Security guards stop them outside and bring them back to the security office. No charges are filed and the merchandise, valued at $44, is recovered undamaged. Since this is Jennifer's first offense, she agrees to complete eight hours of community service as a punishment.

JENNIFER'S CRIME: BURGLARY

Two months later Jennifer and two friends, who are 12- and 13-year-old sisters, enter a house through an unlocked back door. No one is home and they don't have the owner's permission to be there. They had jumped over a back wall to enter the property.

The girls later claim they were looking for money to buy cigarettes. Once inside, though, they see wrapped Christmas presents under the tree. They take some of the presents and open them. Outside the house, they throw the wrappings in a dumpster. They give some of the gifts to friends at school, which creates a trail leading back to them.

After Jennifer is caught, she gives different versions of what happened and who did what. She claims that she took only two dimes from the house. The police investigate and each of the girls is charged with burglary. Some of the items are located and returned to the victims.

Legal Definition of Burglary

A person commits **BURGLARY** by entering or remaining unlawfully in or on a residential structure, a nonresidential structure, a fenced commercial or residential yard, with the intent to commit a theft or any felony thereon.

YOUR CONCERNS AS A JUDGE

Jennifer is 13 when she comes before you on the burglary charge. You can see that she is a bright, articulate young girl. She holds nothing back. She freely admits her involvement in the burglary, after previously claiming she had taken only two dimes. She also admits that she uses drugs. She tells you she wants to start over and not get into any more trouble, but she also finds it hard to resist some of her friends and their negative activities.

You place her on house arrest and send her home with her mother until her sentencing hearing. She is allowed to leave the house only to go to school and for counseling appointments. Her activities are monitored by a probation officer, who makes daily contact in person or by phone.

Jennifer's family history is quite chaotic and has caused her to grow up too fast. Her early use of alcohol, marijuana, crack, speed, and ecstasy is a huge concern. Together with the fact that she likes to steal, something has to be done to protect Jennifer from herself. But can you also help her family?

YOUR SENTENCING OPTIONS AS A JUDGE

Criminal trespass and burglary are property crimes. They don't involve a person getting injured or threatened with harm. Trespass means going on someone's property without their permission. It could include a backyard, the mall if you've been told not to be there, or someone's house. If you trespass with the intent to commit another crime, such as stealing, then you've also committed burglary.

The specific facts of the trespass and burglary incidents usually help you decide the right punishment. If this is a first offense, the punishment may include probation with some community service hours, a class about property crimes, and a letter of apology to the victim. Or the judge may not think probation is necessary, depending on the circumstances. If this is the person's second trespass or burglary, the penalty will be stricter, such as jail time with intensive or standard probation. This is Jennifer's first burglary but second theft, so you can take that history into consideration when deciding an appropriate penalty. The juvenile who continues to break into homes or cars will likely be sent to jail.

Your sentencing options for Jennifer include:
- A few days or weekends in jail, followed by probation.
- Probation with community service and payment to the victim, along with drug counseling and drug testing.

- Placement in a day support program, which provides schooling combined with supervision, and individual and group counseling.
- Placement in residential drug treatment facility.
- Placement in foster care temporarily, while you further investigate what Jennifer needs.
- Anything else?

QUESTIONS TO CONSIDER BEFORE SENTENCING JENNIFER

Write down or discuss your thoughts:
- Does Jennifer need to be punished, provided treatment for her drug abuse, or both? Why?
- Jennifer is only 13. How does her age influence the sentence you give her? Would jail time be too harsh

for her? Or would it send the right message?
- If Jennifer were 16 or 17, would you feel different about her activities? Should we expect a 13-year-old to know about the consequences of shoplifting, breaking into someone's house, and using drugs?
- Jennifer's family is poor and struggling to make ends meet. Should you take that into account? Why or why not?
- Should you get involved in trying to help the family? If so, how?
- Do you think Jennifer should be taken away from her mother and put in foster care temporarily, until her mother can provide a better life? Why or why not?
- Is poverty or a hard life ever an excuse for crime? If so, how? If not, why not?
- Should Jennifer be made to go to school, if the money she makes working helps support her family? A 13-year-old who works is a violation of the child labor laws. Should you look the other way and

not discuss this with Jennifer and her mother in court? What message would that send?

YOU BE THE JUDGE

Complete this sentence:
Based on the information available to me, Jennifer's sentence should be...

WHAT ACTUALLY HAPPENED

Jennifer and her mother appeared at her sentencing. Her attitude was positive, and she said she was sorry for her behavior and was willing to accept whatever I decided.
- I placed her on probation for one year.
- She was to complete 40 community service hours, which she could do at school.

- The victim filed a claim for the stolen items that weren't recovered. I told Jennifer that she and her friend were responsible for this and ordered her to pay her share, which came to $196. This was a great deal of money for Jennifer and her mother. I set a minimum payment of $2 a week until the amount was paid in full. I knew she was poor, but she had been working to help out the family. I also told her that, if done with the right attitude and done well, community service hours could often turn into a paid position after the court-ordered hours are completed. Once Jennifer did her 40 unpaid hours, the school or church where she worked might offer her a part-time job.
- She had to stay away from all drugs, alcohol, and cigarettes, attend drug counseling, and submit to drug testing at her probation officer's direction. If she tested positive for drugs, she would be in violation of her probation and facing jail time.

- She was required to stay in school with no unexcused absences.

At the time of Jennifer's sentencing, an opening in a day support program was unavailable (another example of how a judge can't always give a young person the services she needs). As an alternative, I felt it was necessary to give Jennifer very specific orders about what she was required to do to avoid being locked up.

We had a long way to go with Jennifer. But I let her know that I was concerned about her doing well on probation. She knew she faced jail time if she failed.

I told her mother that Jennifer's job was to stay drug-free and in school. The mother's job was to provide supervision, food, and shelter. It was obvious that Jennifer and her mother were close and that they loved each other. I gave her mother a list of resources if money ran short, including the local food bank and a homeless shelter.

YOUR RESPONSE TO THE JUDGE'S DECISION

Write down or discuss your thoughts:
- Are you surprised by the judge's sentence? Why or why not?
- Was it harder or easier on Jennifer than your sentence? In what ways?
- What part of the judge's sentence do you agree with? What part do you disagree with? Why?
- Is there anything missing from Jennifer's sentence? If so, what is it and why is it important?
- What do you predict will happen to Jennifer?

JENNIFER AFTER SENTENCING

Jennifer did fine on probation for the first six months. She did her community service hours by helping to feed the homeless and cleaning up a local skate park. She remembers how embarrassed she was when some of her friends saw her working there.

Then she stopped going to school and decided to leave the state to live with her father and grandmother. She felt restless and wanted a change. She stayed there for almost a year and held a job, before returning to her mother. Because she was on probation and left without permission of the court, a warrant was issued for her arrest. When she returned, she faced three counts of probation violation: running away, missing school, and not paying money to the burglary victim. Jennifer admitted one of the counts and the others were dropped. She spent 15 hours in jail before returning to her mother's home. She was told that her probation would end once her victim was paid in full.

Letter from Jennifer After Her Release from Jail (age 16)

From then to now
By Jennie

When I was first put in jail, I thought I was cool and my friends would like me more. But then I learned as I got older that being a criminal is something that stays with you for the rest of your life. I missed a lot as a result of my behavior—going out with my friends, having sleepovers, talking on the phone, watching my brothers and sister grow up. All of that I missed out on, because I couldn't get my act together.

I learned so much from losing my freedom. I always fought so hard to be independent and ended up getting the total opposite. Drugs and crime definitely do not pay. I also learned how much my mother loves me. Even after all the terrible things I put her through, she has stuck by my side.

JENNIFER TODAY

After her release from jail, no new charges were filed against Jennifer for the next year and a half. She paid off the money and was successfully released from probation.

Jennifer is now 17, goes to school part-time and works full-time for a glass company. She continues to give her mother money to help out. She lives with her boyfriend, who is also sober and working. Jennifer is committed to living a drug-free life. She attends regular Alcoholics Anonymous (AA) and Narcotics Anonymous meetings, and has a sponsor who is her mentor in the AA program.

Remembering her time in jail, Jennifer recalls the crowded conditions and sleeping on a mattress on the floor. "December was cold, and I kept thinking that I don't belong here. I was scared and had no visitors until my court time." Once in court the following day, Jennifer's greatest regret was "making my mom cry in the courtroom when she saw me shackled." Jennifer stated that she spent so much time being angry at the world that her goal now is to survive, be independent, and have good clean friends. She enjoys photography and would someday like to have her own darkroom. She also enjoys music and may get involved with producing events.

Kids like Jennifer are amazing individuals. In spite of all odds, with the world working against them, they survive. They have an inner strength that guides them over the rough spots. There may be an occasional detour, but more often than not, they get back on track. It's inspiring to see Jennifer working, healthy, and off drugs. She clearly knows that her future is up to her and she intends to make the best of it. When she has her first photography exhibit or musical production, I'll be there.

FINAL THOUGHTS

Write down or discuss your thoughts:
- When Jennifer ran away to her father's house, she didn't get into any more trouble while she was there. Would you have put Jennifer in jail for 15 hours because of that probation violation? Or would you have given her a different punishment?
- Has your family ever had financial problems? How did that affect you?
- Do you know someone like Jennifer, who has made the best of her life despite obstacles? What kept that person going?

Did You Know?

One in six children in America live in poverty—approximately 12 million children. Poverty is defined as a family of three with income less than

$14,000 a year, or a family of four with income less than $18,000 a year (Children's Defense Fund 2002).

JERRY, 15

home break-in and theft

JERRY'S BACKGROUND LEADING UP TO THE CRIME

Jerry has two older brothers and a younger sister. They live together with their mother and stepfather. Jerry was born out of wedlock and does not know his father. His stepfather has been with the family for the past eight years. Although his mother is affectionate and cares about Jerry, she is unable to control him. Jerry doesn't get along with his stepfather and basically ignores him.

Jerry is in special education in grade school for behavior difficulties. He gets into his first serious trouble when he's 12. It's past midnight when he's stopped by the police for violating curfew. He is miles from home without his parents' knowledge or permission. This is the beginning of Jerry's juvenile court career. His brothers have also gotten into trouble with the law, including one incident where the three brothers got into a fight at home and were all arrested.

Because he keeps running away and violating curfew, Jerry gets placed on probation at age 13. He's given standard probation terms, appropriate for his age—attend school, participate in a class about youth and the law, and complete some community service hours. Jerry follows the rules at times, but more often he rebels against all authority. Jerry's mother and stepfather support him, attend all his hearings, and want what's best for him. But he continues to stay out at night and miss school. He has no high school credits and plans to study for his GED. He's never held a steady job, although he bagged groceries for a few weeks. He also has been drinking and smoking marijuana since age 13.

When he's 14, Jerry and two friends are caught breaking windows at a housing project under construction. He's charged with trespass and damaging property. Jerry gets locked up for a month.

> ### Letter from Jerry While in Jail (age 14)
>
> *Judge Thomas A. Jacobs,*
> *I am writing this letter to you because I found out that you didn't want to be mean to me. You just wanted to help me and keep me out of trouble. So I want to thank you. And I don't know if I am going to come to court in a red or yellow shirt, but I am going to try so you know that I am not that bad. But I want to get out of here so I can be with my family and not get in trouble. I am going to do my very best out there. So please, give me another chance. I promise I won't let you down.*
> *Jerry*

Jerry stays on probation after he gets out. A few months later, after caught using marijuana, Jerry is put on intensive probation. This includes house arrest, where he can't leave home except for school, drug testing, and counseling.

Jerry keeps doing whatever he wants. He's brought back to court many times for violating probation. Once he's caught panhandling to get money for drugs. Twice he gets sent to a month-long jail program for kids who violate probation. It includes drug abuse treatment and individual counseling. Finally, when Jerry is 15 and is finished with the program a second time, you tell him that the court has tried everything to help him. He's now 15 and has already spent a total of 1 1/2 years in jail on various offenses. You warn him that his next offense will send him to jail for a long time.

JERRY'S CRIME: BURGLARY AND THEFT

About two months later, a neighbor sees Jerry breaking into a house. When the police arrive, he tries to run away. He's caught with stolen property in his possession. He's arrested and taken to jail. Jerry admits stealing the victim's property in order to get money for drugs. Sentencing is scheduled in your court.

Legal Definitions of Burglary and Theft

A person commits **BURGLARY** by entering or remaining unlawfully in or on a residential structure, a nonresidential structure, a fenced commercial or residential yard, with the intent to commit a theft or any felony therein.

A person commits **THEFT** if, without lawful authority, the person knowingly controls property of another with the intent to deprive the other person of such property.

YOUR CONCERNS AS A JUDGE

Jerry's mother and stepfather are as frustrated as you are with Jerry's behavior. They love him and want what's best for him, even if that means locking him up. But they don't want him to go to jail for a long time because they feel he would be harmed by the experience.

Jerry has been recently evaluated by a psychologist. The report says he uses drugs to self-medicate. He is easily distracted, highly impulsive, and defies authority. The doctor says he needs to be away from his peers and drugs. Jerry is well-behaved when locked up, but he can't control himself when he's out on the streets. Being with his friends is very important to him. But if he is away from them in a drug treatment program, Jerry might be able to turn his life around.

While Jerry hasn't taken probation seriously, he sometimes gives the impression that he wants to change his behavior. However, he hasn't benefited from any of the programs set up for him. It's obvious to you that Jerry is not intimidated by the court. He's made many promises about changing, but hasn't followed through. He feels he can do whatever he wants. Jerry is in danger of becoming a greater risk to the community.

YOUR SENTENCING OPTIONS AS A JUDGE

The burglary charge is dismissed when Jerry admits to the theft. But in sentencing him for the theft, you can still take into account that he broke into someone's house.

> Pleading guilty to one charge in return for dismissal of other charges is common. This is called plea bargaining. It reduces delays in the courts, which are often overcrowded and have many cases to decide.

A theft charge usually results in probation and payment to the victim. Sometimes there's time in jail. But in Jerry's case, other measures should be considered since he's a repeat offender and has a three-year history with the court.

Sentencing options available to you are:

- A lengthy jail term—from 3 to 12 months—as you warned him about at his last sentencing, with drug treatment, counseling, and other services while in jail.
- Commitment to a drug treatment program away from home for at least six months to a year.
- Continued intensive probation with the threat of future jail time if he gets in trouble again, along with

drug treatment, counseling, and payment to the victim.
- Regular probation and payment to the victim.
- Anything else?

QUESTIONS TO CONSIDER BEFORE SENTENCING JERRY

Write down or discuss your thoughts:
- Would you give Jerry another chance before sending him to jail? Why or why not?
- If you don't send Jerry to jail, what makes you think he'll behave differently this time?
- Jerry spent almost two months in jail waiting to be sentenced. Do you think that he might have changed during that time and needs no more additional jail time?

- Should Jerry and his family have intensive counseling? What if he and his family don't want counseling? Can they still benefit from it? Should the court order it anyway?
- Is it possible to change Jerry's rebellious attitude after he's been getting in trouble for years? Why or why not?
- What does Jerry need most to turn his life around?
- What would you say to Jerry at his sentencing? What would you say to his parents?

YOU BE THE JUDGE

Complete this sentence:
Based on the information available to me, Jerry's sentence should be...

WHAT ACTUALLY HAPPENED

Considering Jerry's history of trouble and the seriousness of the recent burglary and theft, I felt it was time for him to settle down in one place for a while. He was at great risk of getting in trouble again if he went home. I was out of options. I sentenced Jerry to:

- Six months in jail, with a recommendation that he be involved in their drug treatment program and individual counseling.

I told him he should think about his sentence as a new beginning. He could make the best of it and then stay away from trouble after he got out.

This wasn't what Jerry wanted to hear and he didn't think I was doing him a favor. But later down the road, he might remember what I said. I told him the jail could keep him longer, depending on how he behaved. It was now up to him.

YOUR RESPONSE TO THE JUDGE'S DECISION

Write down or discuss your thoughts:
- Are you surprised by the judge's sentence? Why or why not?
- Was it harder or easier on Jerry than your sentence? In what ways?
- What part of the judge's sentence do you agree with? What part do you disagree with? Why?
- Is there anything missing from the judge's sentence? What is it and why is it important?
- What do you think will happen to Jerry? Why?

JERRY TODAY

Jerry caused a few problems while in jail. He was slow following the rules and got into arguments with the other kids and staff. As a penalty, his sentence was increased to nine months. On his 16th birthday he was granted parole and returned home to his parents.

Since being paroled, Jerry has stayed out of trouble. He is looking into a GED program and trying to get into an auto mechanics class. He has helped friends fix their cars and wants to try to do it full time.

When he was first locked up for 16 days when he was 13, Jerry hated everything about it: "I couldn't sleep at night—we only had small mats to lay on and no pillow. The food sucked, but the chicken patties were okay." He remembered that the menu never changed whenever he returned to jail.

"It took me eight times to learn not to commit crimes—to learn the real consequences of crime and not to do drugs. I now stay away from drugs and they stay away from me. It's better to have control over your own life, than have someone telling you when you can go to the bathroom."

When asked about what he would tell other teens, Jerry said, "Drugs are fun when you're doing it, but the heartache comes when you're coming off them—and the trouble that it leads to. Listen to your parents—they know what's best. I don't agree with everything my parents say, but I follow them because they know what's right."

FINAL THOUGHTS

Write down or discuss your thoughts:
- Are you surprised Jerry stayed away from trouble and off drugs? Do you

think he'll continue to stay away from crime and drugs?
- Have you or a member of your family ever been robbed or burglarized? Has anyone ever broken into your home? What was the experience like? What was the hardest thing about it?
- If you saw a friend breaking into a neighbor's home, would you call the police or look the other way? Why?
- Has there ever been a time in your life when it seemed that you were in trouble all the time? When you just couldn't do anything right? What was going wrong in your life and why was it happening?
- What was your parents' response to your behavior? Were you grounded or disciplined in any manner? Looking back, what have you learned from the experience?
- Do you know someone like Jerry, who's always getting into trouble? Is there anything you could say or do to help that person out?
- Have you ever spent time in jail? What impact did it have on you?

Did You Know?

Zero Tolerance for Drugs at School in Action

- In 2002, an appellate court in Arizona rejected a request to set aside a school suspension filed by a high school freshman. She was caught giving two classmates Tylenol 3, a prescription drug with codeine. She transferred to an alternative school.

- In 2001, 17-year-old Jessica was suspended for two weeks after school officials found two marijuana stems and a seed in a car she drove to school. She maintained a 3.8 grade-point average and played basketball and softball. She returned after serving her suspension.

- In 2001, 15-year-old Chris was seen at school during lunch giving another student a Vitamin C tablet and a food supplement. He was suspended for 10 days, which was later reduced after a meeting with his parents and school officials.

JOSHUA, 15

cutting school

JOSHUA'S BACKGROUND LEADING UP TO THE CRIME

Joshua is the youngest in his family and the only child who still lives at home. His older sister and two older brothers have moved away. Joshua is being raised by his mother and has little contact with his father. When Joshua is 13, his mother becomes ill and has several surgeries. She takes medication to deal with her chronic pain. As a result of the medication's side effects, she becomes quieter, less attentive to Joshua, and rarely leaves the house. Joshua doesn't fully understand why she's changed or her need to take medication. He and his mother constantly argue over her situation. They get counseling to deal with their arguments, but it doesn't help.

Joshua's contact with law enforcement begins when he's 13. During an argument with his mother, he allegedly throws a book at her and pushes her. His mom calls the police, but since this is his first brush with the law, he is not arrested or taken to court. Instead, Joshua agrees to attend a half-day class of instruction and role-playing about teen behavior, attitudes, and the consequences of making right and wrong decisions.

JOSHUA'S CRIME: TRUANCY

When Joshua is 14, he's still having problems listening to and getting along with his mother. He starts cutting classes and experiments with alcohol and marijuana. Because state law requires that he has to go to school, he is cited by his principal for truancy.

Joshua is given the opportunity to avoid going to court to face a formal truancy charge. He is placed in a diversion program, where he is required to attend a truancy prevention class and complete 20 community service hours. But Joshua fails to go to the class and keeps cutting school. Because he doesn't keep his part of the agreement, he is formally charged with truancy and locked up for the first time to await sentencing.

Joshua is very surprised that afternoon in court when you tell him he won't be going home. You had given him several chances to follow your orders and get back to school, but for whatever reason he ignored them. You set his sentencing in two weeks.

Legal Definition of Truancy

All children between the ages of 6 and 16 are required to attend school. Excused absences, pursuant to the rules of the school district, are permissible. (Each state has its own

> attendance laws. In Wisconsin, children 6 to 18 have to attend school; in Oregon, it's ages 7 to 18.)

YOUR CONCERNS AS A JUDGE

Joshua presents you with a challenge. He has no juvenile record and isn't a hard-core delinquent or a threat to society. He loves his mother but clearly has issues with her use of drugs, even though they are painkillers. She comes to one hearing and is obviously not in good health. She explains that she is heavily medicated and that this affects her ability to parent Joshua. She wants Joshua to come home and obey her. But Joshua doesn't want to live with his mother. He says they can't get along.

You can either send him home and hope he doesn't run away, or grant his request to live with his 22-year-old brother. You met his brother at one of the hearings and know he's genuinely concerned about Joshua. He has offered to take Joshua in and supervise him. But Joshua's brother is on adult probation for drug offenses and is being supervised by the courts himself. You're not sure he can properly supervise Joshua or set a good example in general. But if you send Joshua home to his mother, will they continue to fight?

Joshua is given a psychological evaluation while in jail and the doctor describes him as a confident youth who relates well with others. He is also independent, wants to do things his own way, and is attracted to high-risk situations that border on breaking the law. The doctor recommends he have probation, along with random drug testing.

How can the court best help Joshua?

YOUR SENTENCING OPTIONS AS A JUDGE

Truancy cases are usually handled by the school, which hands out a punishment to the student and the case is then closed. Quite often, the school district and local prosecutor use a diversion program. This means the student admits cutting school and agrees to attend a truancy prevention class and/or complete some community service hours. The youth is not formally charged and the court is not involved.

This would have happened in Joshua's case, but he didn't follow through with his part of the agreement. Now that he's back in court, you intend to make sure that he goes to school and stays in school.

Sentencing options available to you are:

- Jail time, such as a few weekends or during a school vacation, followed by probation.
- Send Joshua to live with his brother and keep him on probation.
- Intensive probation with deferred jail time if Joshua misses school again.
- Regular probation, with counseling for Joshua and his mother and the same community service he missed.
- Case closed, with no jail time or probation, but a warning from the judge.
- Anything else?

QUESTIONS TO CONSIDER BEFORE SENTENCING JOSHUA

Write down or discuss your thoughts:

- Joshua has spent two weeks in jail awaiting sentencing. Should he spend any more time in jail? Or are there better ways to deal with his situation?
- Since Joshua was 13, he has lived with his mother and her medical problems. He says she became a different person following her first surgery. She became quieter, less attentive to Joshua, and rarely left the house. Medication became a part of her daily life. Would more counseling help Joshua understand and accept his mother's condition? It hasn't helped in the past. What can the court do to help Joshua and his mother get at the root of their problems and get along?
- Would you release Joshua to his mother? If so, what can you do to make sure they don't continue to fight?
- Joshua wants to live with his older brother, who is on probation for drug use. Would you allow him to live there?
- Knowing Joshua's attitude toward school, what is the best way to

make sure he goes back to school and stays there?

YOU BE THE JUDGE

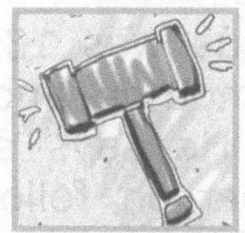

Complete this sentence:
Based on the information available to me, Joshua's sentence should be...

WHAT ACTUALLY HAPPENED

At his sentencing, Joshua was brought into the courtroom by a corrections officer. His mother and brother were also present. Although Joshua was happy to see his family in court, he hesitated when I asked him what he thought I should do.

He said he wanted out of jail. I knew from the reports I read that Joshua didn't want to live with his mother. But he didn't want to hurt his mother by saying this in front of her, so Joshua told me that he wanted to go home and would follow his mother's rules. We talked about his mother's health and her need to follow her doctor's advice and take medication. Joshua said he understood and would try to accept the situation and be more helpful at home. His brother offered to do whatever he could for Joshua, whether he lived with him or their mother.

I didn't feel Joshua needed any more time in jail. I gave him the following sentence:

- I sent him home to his mother and placed him on probation for the next year.
- I also arranged for weekly in-home counseling for both of them.
- I ordered Joshua to stay in school and complete the original 20 hours of community service. Because he had missed the earlier deadline to finish the community service, Joshua thought it would be forgotten. I told him otherwise.

I felt there was a good chance that everything would work out. It was obvious that Joshua's family cared about him. Two weeks in jail was a dose of reality for all of them. I hoped there wouldn't be a need for any more jail time.

YOUR RESPONSE TO THE JUDGE'S DECISION

Write down or discuss your thoughts:
- Are you surprised by the judge's sentence? Why or why not?
- Was it harder or easier on Joshua than your sentence? In what ways?
- What part of the judge's sentence do you agree with? What part do you disagree with? Why?
- Were you surprised that Joshua got locked up in the first place for missing school? Did the court go too far, or was jail the only alternative?

- What do you think will happen to Joshua? Why?

JOSHUA TODAY

I was surprised to learn that Joshua didn't complete his community service hours and started missing school again. He went back to jail for an additional 16 days. This time, Joshua and his mother agreed that it would be better for him to live with his brother, whom Joshua described as his best friend and role model (this surprised me, given his brother's drug history). Joshua had worked with him in the past at a moving company. Although the brother was still on probation, he and Joshua were close and both would be closely supervised by their respective probation officers. I met with the family again and approved the arrangement.

Unfortunately, the brother violated his probation and was sent back to jail. Joshua, now 16, moved to his grandmother's home. This apparently was what Joshua needed. He successfully met all of his probation terms and was granted an early release five months later.

Joshua returned to school and earned his GED at a local community college. He plans to continue his studies in computers or electronics. Between working and spending time with his girlfriend, Joshua enjoys video games, his new Xbox, and working out.

When asked to comment about his jail experience, he said:

"I was pretty scared. I thought, what did I get myself into? I didn't think I'd get locked up for missing school. My time in jail felt like a long time, especially with people constantly telling me what to do.

"Don't expect to have a fun time—I met some pretty weird people in there, some scary kids. The second time I thought how did I do this again—I was stupid and even more immature. It gave me a chance to think about everything. I'm not coming back to this place. I also thought I might lose my girlfriend—that she wouldn't want to be with me now that I was locked up."

Joshua's advice to others: "I would tell kids today to stay away from negative friends and to think ahead, not for the present. What's taking a candy bar, or someone's money, compared to going to jail? Go to school and don't ditch classes. Think about the future, not just about today."

FINAL THOUGHTS

Write down or discuss your thoughts:
- What do you feel was the main cause of Joshua's problems? Could his problems have been handled in a different way by the court?
- Joshua seemed to get his life together once he lived with his grandmother. Should the court have considered that option earlier?
- Has a family member ever suffered from a serious illness? How did it

affect your relationship with that person? With your family as a whole? What was hardest about it?
- Have you ever cut school or dropped out? What made school hard? Were you able to go back? What made you go back?
- Have you ever left home to live with another family member or friend? What made you leave home? Did you go back? Why or why not?

Did You Know?

Thinking of dropping out? Well, look at these figures:

- The unemployment rate in 2000 among dropouts was 28 percent compared to 12 percent for those who finished high school.

- Now consider these average annual salaries (1999* and 2000 figures):

	females	males
Less than a ninth grade education*:	$10,754	$16,704
Some high school but no diploma:	$11,583	$19,225
High school diploma or GED:	$16,573	$26,399
Some college:	$21,597	$31,336
Four-year college degree:	$32,238	$42,292

(National Center for Education Statistics, 2001)

MARCUS, 14

stealing a telephone cord

MARCUS'S BACKGROUND LEADING UP TO THE CRIME

Marcus lives with his mother, an older brother, and a younger sister. His father lives out of state and has little contact with Marcus. He is a freshman in high school and his behavior at school and in the community is good. Marcus has never been in trouble with the law. He is on the honor roll and he participates in basketball, football, and swimming. His mother calls Marcus a model teenager. He is not involved with drugs or alcohol, and his mother knows and approves of his friends. His older brother is a prison guard, and his sister is in school and also plays sports.

MARCUS'S CRIME: SHOPLIFTING

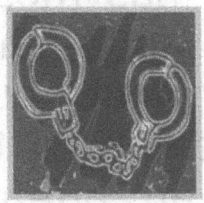

Marcus, 14, is in a store. A security guard sees him take a phone cord from a shelf, remove it from the package, and hide it in his jacket pocket. He puts the empty package back on the shelf and walks away. When he goes past the cash register without making any attempt to pay for the cord, he is stopped by security. Marcus denies doing anything wrong and the police are called. He's held by the police for about a half hour before being taken home. Marcus tells his mother that he didn't do anything wrong and that he wants to plead not guilty to the shoplifting charge. His lawyer explains to Marcus that he will have to go to trial and the court will decide whether he's guilty or not. As a first-time offender, Marcus stays home awaiting trial.

A teenager has most of the same rights as an adult in the criminal justice system. Under our Constitution, everyone has the right to a trial when charged with an offense. If a teen says he or she is innocent of a charge, a trial will be scheduled and the state has to prove beyond a reasonable doubt that the teen is guilty. At any time during the proceedings the teen may change his or her mind and admit the charge or accept the state's plea offer, if it is still available to them. If found guilty at trial or by admitting the charge, a sentencing hearing is then scheduled.

Legal Definition of Shoplifting

A person commits **SHOPLIFTING** if, while in an establishment in which merchandise is displayed for sale, such person knowingly obtains such goods of another, with the intent to deprive that person of such goods by

> removing the goods without paying for them, or by concealing (hiding) the goods.

YOUR CONCERNS AS A JUDGE

When you see Marcus and his mother in court for his trial five months later, you have the impression that he never thought things would go this far. He looks surprised when he sees the store manager and police officer that arrested him. That's when it hits him that this is for real and that everyone takes the incident seriously. His attorney asks for a few minutes to talk with Marcus before the trial begins. The attorney then announces that Marcus has changed his mind and wants to avoid a trial by admitting what he did.

Marcus tells you he knows he made a mistake. He says he didn't admit it right away because he didn't want to disappoint his mother, who has a high opinion of him. Now he wants to take responsibility.

> Pleading not guilty and then admitting guilt later does not increase the penalty. Whether Marcus pled guilty at first or was found guilty following a trial, the penalty would be the same.

YOUR SENTENCING OPTIONS AS A JUDGE

Shoplifting is stealing—there is no way around it. Stiff penalties may be imposed if the value of the stolen merchandise is over $250. If less than that amount, as in this case, the crime may be handled differently.

This is Marcus's first offense and the phone cord was valued at only a few dollars. Now you have to decide the penalty.

Sentencing options available to you are:
- A short jail sentence, ranging from a week to a weekend, followed by probation, ranging from a minimum of three months to a maximum of one year.
- Probation for up to one year, including community service hours, a class about shoplifting and its penalties, and a letter of apology to the store owner.
- Probation with no other terms.
- Prohibit Marcus from entering any store unless his mother is with him.
- Order Marcus to pay a fine.
- Issue him a warning and close the case.
- Anything else?

QUESTIONS TO CONSIDER BEFORE SENTENCING MARCUS

Write down or discuss your thoughts:
- When Marcus was caught shoplifting, he spent a few hours with the police before being taken home. He also had to appear in court, where he admitted his guilt. Has Marcus been punished enough? Should his case be closed, or should he be given additional punishment?
- Marcus did not admit he shoplifted until five months later. Does that affect the sentence you give him? Why or why not?
- Should he be prohibited from entering any store unless he's with his mother? Why or why not?
- Marcus is a first offender who committed a relatively minor crime.

But if you don't punish him, he may do more serious crimes in the future. What's the best approach to take?

YOU BE THE JUDGE

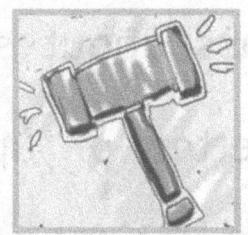

Complete this sentence:
Based on the information available to me, Marcus's sentence should be...

WHAT ACTUALLY HAPPENED

It took Marcus a while, but he did the right thing in admitting what he had done. I understood that he had lied to protect his mother. But I was concerned that he denied the crime for five months. Marcus needed to understand that everyone makes mistakes and that it's better to admit them rather than lie about them. I thought Marcus needed

to be held accountable for his behavior. I ordered Marcus to:
- Probation for one year, with an early release if he followed all his terms.
- Complete 30 hours of community service.
- Take a class about shoplifting and the law.
- Write a letter of apology to the store.

I was confident that the sentence was appropriate. Marcus impressed me as someone who I wouldn't see in court again.

YOUR RESPONSE TO THE JUDGE'S DECISION

Write down or discuss your thoughts:
- Are you surprised by the judge's sentence? Why or why not?

- Was it harder or easier on Marcus than your sentence? In what ways?
- What part of the judge's sentence do you agree with? What part do you disagree with? Why?
- Do you think Marcus will shoplift or get into trouble again?

Letter of Apology from Marcus to the Store Owner (age 14)

Dear Sir/Madam,

My name is Marcus. I tried to steal a telephone cord from your store. I don't know why I did it, because I know it is wrong to steal. My mother has always taught me that if I want something bad enough, I can earn the money to buy it. I hate the pain I see in my mother's eyes because I know that I caused it. I hate the guilt that I feel, but I caused that too. I hate the example that I set for my little sister because I am supposed to be a role model for her. I am very ashamed of myself, and I promise

you that I will never try to steal anything ever again.
   Sincerely,
   Marcus

Letter from the Store Owner to Marcus

Dear Marcus:
I received your letter and was quite impressed. It takes a brave person to admit when they have made a big mistake. You accepted responsibility for your actions and now realize that when you do something like this, it hurts others. I hope you always think of the consequences of your actions and make the right choices. I wish you the best of luck.
   Sincerely,
   Frank R.
   Store Director

MARCUS TODAY

Marcus had no probation violations. He was allowed to complete his community service at school, cleaning classrooms and the school grounds. The owner of the store had no objection to an early release from probation, which was granted when Marcus was 15. He has had no further contact with the court or law enforcement.

Marcus is now 18 and a senior in high school. He has maintained good grades and has stayed active in sports. He is eligible for a basketball scholarship and plans to attend college as a business major. Marcus has a collection of sports trophies proudly displayed at home.

His reaction to the incident, as expressed in his letter, was overwhelming shame and disappointment. "Put yourself in your parents' position, and how they would react—very disappointed. I was a good son—they raised me better than that."

FINAL THOUGHTS

Write down or discuss your thoughts:
- What would you do if you and your friend went into a store and your friend shoplifts? Would you say something to her? Why or why not? Do you think you would remain friends? Why or why not?
- Have you ever been tempted to shoplift? If so, what happened? If not, why not?
- Have you ever been caught up in a lie or deception? Did things get out of control as the lie grew? How did you resolve the problem? Or are you still living with it?
- What Marcus did is a clear case of shoplifting. Which of the following is considered shoplifting:

- Switching price tags on an item and paying the lower price when you leave the store.
- Opening a bag of candy and eating one piece.
- Putting an item in your pocket, intending to steal it, but changing your mind and putting it back on the shelf.
- Being a lookout for a friend who is shoplifting.

Answer: Depending on where you live, all four examples could be shoplifting. It's up to the police and prosecutor to decide how to handle each case.

Did You Know?

In 1999, there were over one million shoplifting incidents reported in the United States, with an average stolen amount of $165.

NATALIE, 14

caught with beer at a party

NATALIE'S BACKGROUND LEADING UP TO THE CRIME

Natalie is one of five children. She lives with her parents, three brothers, and a sister. She is a good student with lots of friends. She joins the track team and works on the school yearbook. She also participates in a local civic group, working with homeless children.

Natalie comes home late a couple of times and cuts a few classes. However, she is never cited for curfew violations or truancy. Her parents deal with these incidents as they occur, either by grounding her or taking away her phone privileges.

NATALIE'S CRIME: UNDERAGE POSSESSION OF ALCOHOL

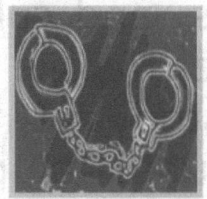

It is 2A.M. when Natalie's parents are awakened by a call from the police. They are asked to come and pick up their 14-year-old daughter at her friend's house.

Earlier that day, Natalie receives her parents' permission to spend the night at Christy's house. But Natalie doesn't mention that Christy's parents are out of town for the weekend. Word spreads quickly and it isn't long before a loud and crowded party is underway.

After several calls from upset neighbors, the police come and break up the party. Partygoers are charged with a variety of offenses, including curfew violations, possession and consumption of alcohol, disturbing the peace, property damage, and resisting arrest. Natalie, along with some of her friends, is given a ticket for possession of beer.

It takes almost two hours for the police to break up the party, question each of the kids, and call their parents. During that time, Natalie and her friends are in the custody of the police and cannot leave until a parent arrives. Natalie's parents ground her as a punishment, until her hearing in court—she must stay home unless in school or with her parents.

Legal Definition of Possession of Alcohol

It is unlawful for a person who is under the legal drinking age of 21 to **POSSESS, CONSUME, PURCHASE, OR SELL SPIRITUOUS LIQUOR.** This provision does not prohibit minors from working under the supervision of an adult, in grocery stores where the minor may package or carry out spirituous liquor in unbroken packages for the convenience of the customer.

> In all states the legal drinking age is 21, but some states have exceptions for special family events (a glass of wine at dinner with your parents) or religious ceremonies. But to buy, possess, and consume alcohol in the usual sense, the legal age is 21.

YOUR CONCERNS AS A JUDGE

Natalie's case is not unusual. Thousands of teens are cited every weekend for alcohol offenses. Teens either have access to an empty house or apartment, or they get together at some remote location. Sometimes the police get wind of the party and it's broken up. Depending on the charge, some teens simply pay a fine and the case is closed. Others may face additional penalties, depending on the circumstances.

In deciding what to do in these cases, you consider the juvenile's attitude, as well as the attitude of the parents. If the juvenile doesn't think she did anything wrong and is annoyed at being in court, the penalty may be more severe. On the other hand, if the young person is sorry, and the parents are concerned and have already disciplined their child, then the penalty would be less severe. If the young person admits having a problem with alcohol and asks for help, that is a good sign.

You know that Natalie does not have a juvenile record. She admits being at the party and drinking some beer. She understands she broke the law and seems sorry. What should her sentence be to make sure she doesn't make the same mistake again?

YOUR SENTENCING OPTIONS AS A JUDGE

Penalties for possession or consumption of alcohol vary around the country. Judges have to take into account a number of factors, including the age of the offender, whether this is a first offense, and available resources. Attendance at an alcohol awareness class may be all that is needed for a first-time offender. (This class generally covers the local drinking laws and includes role playing, discussion, and debate about drinking and drug abuse.) A juvenile with a drinking problem may be required to go to Alcoholics Anonymous meetings, drug testing, and be monitored during a probation period. Each case is handled individually according to the juvenile's history and needs.

Sentencing options available to you are:
- Jail time for a weekend or a few hours, followed by probation for one to three months.
- Probation for one to three months, community service, and a letter on what she learned from this experience.
- An alcohol awareness class and a fine of $100.
- An alcohol awareness class and community service hours.
- Require Natalie to write a letter on what she learned from the experience and close the case.
- Give Natalie a warning and close the case without any further punishment.
- Anything else?

QUESTIONS TO CONSIDER BEFORE SENTENCING NATALIE

Write down or discuss your thoughts:
- Do you think Natalie should be given a few hours or maybe a weekend in jail? Would that be a valuable lesson not only to her, but also to her friends? Why or why not?
- Natalie is a first-time offender who was caught drinking beer. You could go easy on her. But if you don't, there's the possibility she might continue to drink and go on to do worse things. What do you do?
- Was getting caught and being with the police enough of a lesson for Natalie? Should the case be dropped? Why or why not?

YOU BE THE JUDGE

Complete this sentence:
Based on the information available to me, Natalie's sentence should be...

WHAT ACTUALLY HAPPENED

Natalie appeared in court with her parents. She decided to admit her guilt and agreed to proceed immediately to sentencing. I discussed the situation with them and gave Natalie the following sentence:
- Probation for three months.
- Complete 20 community service hours, preferably in a hospital emergency room, where Natalie could see firsthand how alcohol abuse hurts people.
- Write a letter about what she learned from this experience.

I wanted to make sure that Natalie understood she would be held accountable for her actions. A brief period of probation was all the situation called for, assuming Natalie stayed out of trouble.

YOUR RESPONSE TO THE JUDGE'S DECISION

Write down or discuss your thoughts:
- Are you surprised by the judge's sentence? Why or why not?
- Was it harder or easier on Natalie than your sentence? In what ways?
- What part of the judge's sentence do you agree with? What part do you disagree with? Why?
- Were probation and the other penalties too harsh for such a minor offense? Why or why not?

Letter that Natalie was Required to Write (age 14)

Dear Judge,

I'm writing this letter because you told me to write down what I learned from getting caught at a party with beer. I cannot stop thinking about the night at my friend's party and what a disaster it ended up being. When the cops first arrived at my friend's house, I was thinking it was such a buzzkill for them to break up the party. But as they approached the house, we knew that we were about to get into serious trouble.

I had a horrible feeling in the pit of my stomach as I heard the cops pounding on the door and shining their flashlights through the windows. Everyone in the house was scared out of their minds as the cops entered the kitchen and handcuffed my friend. Her parents were gone for the weekend, so they were taking her to jail. It was so horrible to be waiting in the living room for them to deal with us one by one and see my friend sitting there handcuffed. I didn't know what was going to happen to the rest of us. All I could do was sit there and wait. It seemed like forever.

Then I found out that they were calling everyone's parents to come pick us up. It was about 1:30 in the morning, and I knew my dad would be mad. I don't want to go through anything like this ever again. Any fun I had at the party was not worth those countless minutes of sitting on that couch in complete agony. I plan to listen to my mom and dad and not drink again until I am old enough.

Sincerely,
Natalie

NATALIE TODAY

Natalie followed all of her terms and was off probation early. She has had no further incidents with the law. She went to college and majored in criminal justice, graduated with honors, and traveled for two years before returning to graduate school. In her spare time, Natalie enjoys running and yoga. Her dogs, Bow and Casers, usually run with her.

Natalie suggests that teens try to think 10 years ahead about how getting into trouble might affect the future: "Every kid has a chance to become President, or go into politics, or whatever. Trouble can change all that forever. It's not worth it."

FINAL THOUGHTS

Write down or discuss your thoughts:
- If you knew you could be locked up for a weekend, would you think twice before drinking?

- Is it fair for parents to discipline a teen if he or she also has to go to court for the offense? Why or why not?
- Natalie committed a relatively minor offense. In cases like these, whose responsibility is it to see that the laws are followed—the parents, the police, or the courts? Or all of these?
- Have you ever violated your parents' trust? Were you caught? How did it feel later, after thinking about it? Is your behavior important to younger brothers and sisters? Do you feel an obligation to set an example for them?
- Does it concern you that so many kids get caught with alcohol, with little or no consequences? Shouldn't the court do something to prevent these problems? For example, should judges go out into the community and talk about these issues at schools and parent meetings?
- What would you do if:
  - Some of your friends told other kids to come to your house

on a night when your parents weren't home?

• Some friends came over to hang out with you and they brought alcohol into your home?

• Your only ride home from a party is with your friend, he or she has been drinking beer, and your friend says the beer was not enough to affect his or her driving?

Did You Know?

• In 2000, there were 42,700 juveniles arrested for being drunk, with 21,000 of these for driving under the influence.

• Over 4 million teenagers in America have serious problems with alcohol.

• Approximately 30 percent of boys and 20 percent of girls classify themselves as drinkers by age 12.

• Every year, over 3,000 teenagers are killed in drunk-driving crashes.

(Sources: National Safety Council; SADD; Statistical Abstract of the U.S. 2001)

OLIVIA, 14

a stolen car

OLIVIA'S BACKGROUND LEADING UP TO THE CRIME

Olivia lives with her mother and younger sister. Her mother works during the day while the girls are in school. Olivia's parents divorced when she was 2 and her father lives in another state. She has little contact with him. Olivia also has an adult brother who lives away from home. Her mother's boyfriend lives with them and Olivia says they get along by basically staying out of each other's way.

At 13, Olivia starts running away from home—first for a few hours, then for days at a time. She goes to friends' homes and hangs out until she decides to return. She says everything at home is fine, but sometimes she's bored and just wants to do her own thing and be with her friends. Her mother doesn't know what to do about Olivia's behavior, which is starting to rub off on her younger sister. The mother agrees to counseling for the girls, but doesn't think she needs to be in counseling with them.

One night, after running away, Olivia takes a taxi home but she doesn't have any money and can't pay the fare. She offers the driver her locket and necklace instead of cash. The driver won't accept them and calls the police. Olivia is charged with theft of services, running away, and violation of curfew. She admits the theft and the other charges are dismissed. Both Olivia and her 10-year-old sister, who was with her that night, are locked up. The sister is released the next morning. But Olivia's mother doesn't want Olivia home right away because of her behavior and the effect she is having on her sister. Olivia is kept in jail for three weeks, then is released to her mother and put on probation.

OLIVIA'S CRIME: AUTO THEFT

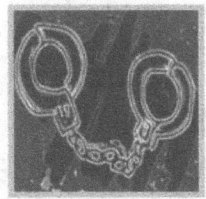

A few weeks later, after graduating from the 8th grade, Olivia and a girlfriend steal a car and leave the state. They hit a wall and damage the car before abandoning it. She makes her way to her father's home, where she stays for four months. Then, to her credit, Olivia decides to return to her mother's home, turn herself in, and accept responsibility. She says she knows she did wrong, wants to pay for the damage to the car, and has learned her lesson.

Oliva is charged with auto theft and she is held in jail for 30 days until her next hearing before you.

Legal Definition of Auto Theft

A person commits **AUTO THEFT** if, without lawful authority, the person knowingly controls another person's means of transportation, with the intent to permanently deprive the person of such means of transportation, or controls another person's means of transportation knowing, or having reason to know, that the property is stolen.

The difference between auto theft and joyriding is a question of intent. If you were only taking the car to use temporarily (drive around the block or keep for a short time) then it's the lesser crime of joyriding. If you plan to take the car permanently, it's auto theft.

YOUR CONCERNS AS A JUDGE

You're surprised to see Olivia again, especially so soon after placing her on probation for not paying the cab fare. She is always very polite in court and seems to have the support of her family. She says that she didn't want to remain with her father, but was afraid to return home right away because she didn't want to be locked up again.

You have psychological reports stating that Olivia acts in a thoughtful manner and that she is capable of changing her behavior. Her probation officer says Olivia is bright and well-spoken. She has no trouble in school when she goes.

However, she runs away so much that it makes it difficult for anyone to work with her. Olivia likes to do as she pleases and go her own way, regardless of the law. And her behavior is getting worse—she just committed a serious crime. You need to consider a new approach to get her attention. She has already spent three weeks in jail on a previous offense, but did she learn her lesson? Maybe it's time to consider intensive probation with daily supervision, or perhaps a six-month residential treatment program where she could receive intensive counseling. Or is it time for a lengthy jail sentence?

How do you impress upon her that she can't run away whenever she wants? That she can't just steal someone's car and leave the state? How do you find out what makes her do these things? What sentence would prevent Olivia from getting into trouble again?

YOUR SENTENCING OPTIONS AS A JUDGE

Car theft is so common across the United States that the prisons would be bursting at the seams if every adult car thief was imprisoned on the first offense for a lengthy period. Many first-time offenders are sent to jail for a few months, while the repeat offender is given longer jail time. Juveniles are dealt with in a similar manner, with increased penalties each time he or she steals another car. For the first-time juvenile car thief, punishment may mean probation and restitution (payment to the victim), but serious consideration would be given to at least a short time in jail. Olivia could be facing some jail time, especially considering her runaway history, and because this car theft happened while she was already on probation.

Your sentencing options include:
- A jail sentence of between three to six months, followed by one year of probation.
- A shorter jail sentence of one month, with one year of probation.
- Commitment to a residential treatment facility for 30 days to six months.
- Intensive probation, payment to the victim, family counseling, and random drug tests.
- Intensive probation, with an electronic ankle bracelet to monitor her whereabouts for the first few months.

- Regular probation, with counseling and payment to the victim for damage to the car.
- Anything else?

QUESTIONS TO CONSIDER BEFORE SENTENCING OLIVIA

Write down or discuss your thoughts:
- Auto theft is a more serious crime than running away or not paying a cab fare. Jail and probation haven't seemed to work with Olivia. What will it take to get her attention and cooperation?
- Should Olivia be sent to jail for six months? Do you think this would help her to grow up and be more responsible when released? Or is this too harsh for a 14-year-old?

- Should Olivia be ordered to pay for the damage to the car she stole? Should a 14-year-old be expected to pay anything back?
- Do you think Olivia is reacting to her family life? Although she says her mother means everything to her, why does she run away? How can the court try to help the family? For example, should the court order family counseling? What does this family need, in your opinion?
- What can you say to Olivia at sentencing that might make a difference?

YOU BE THE JUDGE

Complete this sentence:
Based on the information available to me, Olivia's sentence should be...

WHAT ACTUALLY HAPPENED

After spending 30 days in jail awaiting her hearing, Olivia returned to court for sentencing on the car theft charge. She was wearing a red shirt when she walked into the courtroom, which told me that she had no violations while in jail. (Red is the highest level for kids in jail.) I told her I was glad to see her in red, but it only meant that she could follow the rules when locked up. I told Olivia that the real test would come when she was released. Could she maintain her good behavior once home?

Olivia made all the usual promises, but she said she meant it this time. I explained to her that I would let her go home, but with increased supervision. I gave her the following sentence:

- I placed her on intensive probation for six months, which included daily contact with her probation officer and a surveillance officer who would keep track of her whereabouts. If Olivia followed all the rules she

would be placed on standard probation with less supervision.
- She and her mother were also ordered to pay the victim about $4,000 for the damaged car. Olivia was primarily responsible, but her mother could help her pay it off. Payments were to be made each month, and Olivia had until her 18th birthday to pay it off in full. If the payments weren't made, the victim had the right to sue Olivia and her mother for the money. I knew that Oliva didn't have a job and that her mother was just getting by, but Olivia could baby-sit now and, as she got older, find other jobs to pay her debts. She knew that it was her responsibility and agreed to start making payments.
- I arranged for family counseling and Olivia agreed to participate.
- She was also required to take a drug test whenever her probation officer requested. I had some suspicion that she was experimenting with drugs but no evidence, and Olivia denied it. But

she agreed to the random tests and said she would be clean.

YOUR RESPONSE TO THE JUDGE'S DECISION

Write down or discuss your thoughts:
- Are you surprised by the judge's sentence? Why or why not?
- Was it harder or easier on Olivia than your sentence? In what ways?
- What part of the judge's sentence do you agree with? What part do you disagree with? Why?
- What do you think about the judge ordering her to pay the victim for the damaged car? Is that fair? Or will it make things worse for Olivia? Is it fair to order her mother to help make the payments? Why or why not?

- What do you think will happen to Olivia? Why?

OLIVIA AFTER SENTENCING

Olivia stayed out of trouble for a few months. Then she ran away from home again and was gone for several weeks. She was caught with a small quantity of crystal meth. I was now out of options for Olivia—she wouldn't stay put long enough for any program or counseling to have an effect. This time I sent her to jail for a minimum of four months. Another option would have been to send her to a secure residential treatment facility that she could not run away from, but no spaces were available at the time.

Letter from Olivia While in Jail (age 15)

Dear Judge Jacobs,
I've had a lot of time to think about my behavior and the poor choices I have made. I have hurt many people, myself included. I finally came to understand the damage I have caused to myself

and others. Some of this hurt can be repaired. However, some cannot.

During my current stay in jail, I have taken steps to help heal some of this pain. The first step was coming to realize how it affected my family. The second step has been working on communicating better with my family through writing letters to my mom and stepdad, and visiting with my mom twice a week. I feel that we have grown closer.

The third step I have taken is realizing what a negative impact drugs have had on my life. I've participated in a substance abuse program in jail and have realized that I had been repeatedly making the wrong choices about how to deal with my problems, which made the pain worse, not better.

The fourth step has been completing my education by studying for my G.E.D. The final step I have taken is becoming more aware of what is really going

> *to make me happy, and that's being with my family. I have learned to change the things that I can change and to accept the things I cannot change. Thank you for your sympathy and consideration.*
>
> *Sincerely,*
> *Olivia*

Olivia had participated in everything available to her in jail. She did well enough to be paroled to a residential transition home. She stayed there for a month before going home to her mother.

She started the 9th grade and obeyed her parole terms. Unfortunately, her good behavior didn't last. She was caught with crystal meth again and a pipe. She admitted that both were hers. I placed Olivia in a drug treatment center for three months. She successfully completed the program and returned home. She was required to participate in an outpatient drug treatment program.

However, Olivia soon ran away again and another warrant was issued. She was eventually picked up and spent an additional six months in jail. She studied culinary arts and a maintenance program, where she learned about air conditioning, painting, and hanging drywall. She also earned her GED. She went home from jail five months before her 18th birthday. She had no further incidents or parole violations, and by the time Olivia turned 18 she was free from the juvenile system.

OLIVIA TODAY

She now lives at home with her mother and sister. She works in sales at a department store and is considering going back to school. Olivia enjoys reading and writing in her journal. She is interested in cosmetology and mortuary science. She enjoys being with people and listening to what others have to say. She's going to take her time to decide what's next, and then "go for it. Before, I did things because everyone wanted me to, but now I want to do things for myself, because I want to, not have to."

Although it occurred years ago, Olivia clearly remembers her first stay in jail when she was 13. "A lot of people think it's cool to be locked up, but it's not. I had a bad feeling, but I made the best of it. I couldn't sleep the first night—I was worried about my sister, who was across the hall, and probably crying.

"When you're home, you take everything for granted—little things, like a toilet without a metal seat and good food."

Looking back, Olivia said she had "no regrets, or I wouldn't be what I am today—I dug my hole deep and wanted to get out."

When a young child comes before the court for a minor offense, that experience is usually enough to get his or her attention. Most juveniles who end up in juvenile court don't return. The court experience, combined with parental discipline, results in a small number of repeat appearances.

Then there are kids like Olivia—smart, articulate, yet stubborn and independent at an early age. Courts often bend over backwards to help these young people settle down. Some, as in Olivia's case, take longer for the message to penetrate. When it does, the world is a different place. As Olivia said when she was 18: "Think what I could do if I tried more—if my eyes had been opened earlier." Olivia, it's not too late.

FINAL THOUGHTS

Write down or discuss your thoughts:
- Were you surprised about the way Olivia behaved, after being given a second chance by being put on probation for the stolen car? Should she have been given a tougher sentence after she stole the car?

- Each time the judge saw Olivia in court, it became more frustrating. He knew what she was capable of, but didn't know how to motivate her to change. Why is it so hard to reach young people like Olivia? Would you have been more or less patient with Olivia? Why?
- As Olivia got older, she seemed to settle down. How do time and maturity make a difference?
- Have you ever been the victim of a property crime (theft, burglary, or damage to your property)? What did you want to see happen to the person who committed the crime? Pay you back? Go to jail? Or forget about it and let him or her go free?
- If you've been the victim of a crime, does it make any difference to you if the person who did it was a young person or an adult? Why or why not?

Did You Know?

In 2000, there were 50,800 juveniles arrested for car theft in the United States. Eighty-three percent of those arrested were males, 17 percent were girls, and 26 percent were under age 15.

PHILIP, 9

assault against his mother

PHILIP'S BACKGROUND LEADING UP TO THE CRIME

Philip is the youngest of three children and lives with his mother. His parents are divorced and he has little contact with his father, who reportedly used drugs and spent time in prison. Philip's mother also used drugs when he was younger. She is now drug-free, claiming to have zero tolerance for drugs. Philip has chores to do around the house (washing the dishes, taking out the trash) and usually gets them done, although he isn't crazy about cleaning up after his pets. Philip likes Nintendo, riding his bike, and fishing.

Philip doesn't like school and often refuses to go. A few incidents with school bullies haven't helped. He failed one grade and then switched to a smaller, alternative school. He takes medication because of his hyperactive behavior, but his mother can't always afford to buy it.

PHILIP'S CRIME: ASSAULT

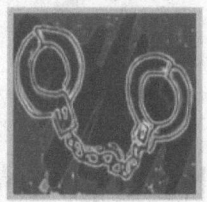

One night, when Philip is 9 and in the 4th grade, he and his mother get into an argument. He begins to swear at his mother and call her names. She takes him to the bathroom to wash his mouth out with soap. Philip turns around and spits in her face. She calls the police and they question Philip. He admits everything. Philip is arrested and taken to jail at 10:30 that night. He spends two hours locked up. He is sorry about what happened and agrees to work on his temper. Philip is sent home with his mother after midnight and told to obey and respect her, and cooperate with the probation officer assigned to his case.

Each state sets its own minimum age for a child to be sent to jail or juvenile detention. In some states the youngest age is 8, while in others it's 10 or 12. Unfortunately for Philip, he lived in a state where a child as young as 8 could be locked up.

Legal Definition of Assault

A person commits **ASSAULT** by intentionally, knowingly, or recklessly causing any physical injury to another person; intentionally placing another person in reasonable apprehension of physical injury; or knowingly touching another person with the intent to injure, insult, or provoke such person.

YOUR CONCERNS AS A JUDGE

There is always a concern when someone as young as Philip is brought to court. Even though the law in some states allows 8-year-olds to be charged with a crime, it is a rare event. So when 9-year-old Philip is brought to jail by the police, everyone involved pays close attention to his situation. Should he remain overnight until he sees a judge the next morning? Or can he calm down enough to go home and obey his mother? If kept in jail, would the experience harm him because he's so young? Or would the stay have a positive effect on his future behavior?

Because Philip promises to listen to his mother and control his temper, you allow him to go home after two hours in jail. In the meantime he will meet with a probation officer, who will make recommendations to you about services for Philip and his family, such as counseling. There is no suspicion or evidence of drug use by Philip or his mother, but perhaps they can get help to stop their fights. You tell Philip when you release him that you don't want to remove him from his home, and that his behavior from this point forward will help you decide his case. If he acts up again before his next hearing, you will have to take that into consideration.

You have the opportunity to keep a young child, soon to be a teenager, out of long-term involvement with the court system. What can you offer Philip and his mother to assist and support them, and to make sure he doesn't come back to jail?

YOUR SENTENCING OPTIONS AS A JUDGE

There are different degrees of assault. If you hit someone and cause an injury, this is an assault. If done with a weapon (knife, gun, rock, etc.), it may be aggravated assault, which carries a greater penalty. But if you touch someone with the intent to insult that person, or upset them to the point where they would strike back, this may also be an assault. Penalties range from unsupervised probation to jail time.

In Philip's case, spitting in his mother's face was an insulting and highly disrespectful action, but she was not physically injured. At sentencing you have the following options available to you:

- A weekend in jail with probation afterwards.
- Intensive probation with deferred jail time, if Philip gets into more trouble.
- Regular probation, with community service, family counseling, drug testing, and a letter of apology to his mother.
- Anger management classes and individual counseling.

- Issue a warning to Philip and close the case.
- Anything else?

QUESTIONS TO CONSIDER BEFORE SENTENCING PHILIP

Write down or discuss your thoughts:
- Were Philip's few hours in jail enough for a 9-year-old, or should he spend a weekend there? Would additional time in jail for such a young child be harmful?
- The mother's behavior has not been very positive in the past—she used drugs. Does this affect the sentence you give Philip? Why or why not?
- Should you try to help Philip and his mother get along better? What could you do to help the family? What, if anything, should be done

to help Philip learn to control his temper?
- Do you think that a judge should always hand out a punishment, no matter what the person's age and circumstances? Or are there times when no punishment is needed?

YOU BE THE JUDGE

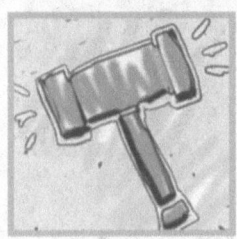

Complete this sentence:
Based on the information available to me, Philip's sentence should be...

WHAT ACTUALLY HAPPENED

Philip returned to court with his mother. All reports about him at home and school were positive. He had followed through on his promises and I felt satisfied that we were headed in the right direction. Philip's attitude in court was positive and his willingness to stay out of trouble was convincing.

But I didn't want to cut him loose just yet. Both Philip and his mother needed assistance from the court. They were poor, so counseling at their expense was out of the question. I arranged for family counseling at Philip's home to be paid by the court.

> All juvenile courts are limited in what they can offer a juvenile and the family. Depending on the size and economic status of your community, the court may not have adequate funds to pay for programs young people need, as was done in Philip's case. It is frustrating for everyone involved when a need exists but there's no money to address the need. A good example of this is the limited funds available nationwide for juvenile sex-offender programs (where kids who have abused others get intensive treatment) or to help runaways.

I placed Philip on probation for up to one year, with a chance for early release upon good behavior at home with his mother. He was required to:

- Complete 10 community service hours, either at school or somewhere else supervised by his mother.
- Take a drug test when told to by his probation officer.
- Write a letter of apology to his mother.

He had 30 days to complete his community service hours and write the letter. I told him that if he continued to do well, I would release him from probation in a few months. If he didn't, he might be facing some jail time in the future.

I thought the threat of more jail time would keep him on track. I didn't expect to see Philip again.

YOUR RESPONSE TO THE JUDGE'S DECISION

Write down or discuss your thoughts:
- Are you surprised by the judge's sentence? Why or why not?
- Was it harder or easier on Philip than your sentence? In what ways?
- What part of the judge's sentence do you agree with? What part do you disagree with? Why?
- Is there something missing from the judge's decision? What is it, and why do you think it is important?

PHILIP AFTER SENTENCING

Philip started out doing fine. He went to school, was always clean on his drug tests, and listened to his mother.

But then Philip, now 11, was caught shoplifting from a store. He admitted what he did, spent three weeks in jail, and was kept on probation. He was ordered to take a class about the crime of shoplifting. Shortly after, though, he was caught shoplifting a bird from a pet store. Again, a few more weeks in jail.

After he was released, Philip followed the rules for almost a year. He ran away a few times and violated his probation, but the stealing had stopped. Yet a new problem came up. Philip, now 13, was using marijuana. It seemed that he had first started smoking pot when he was 10, after his mother introduced him to it. She had since stopped using the drug and wanted Philip to stay clean as well. But Philip was caught with marijuana and spent three weeks in jail for drug possession.

Letter from Philip While in Jail (age 13)

Dear Judge Jacobs,

While in jail I did a lot of thinking. I've been thinking about going home on the 19th of December, and starting all over again. If you let me go home I will go on the right path to be successful in life. I don't want to be a burn-out, like some people who smoke pot everyday. I would like to put an end to it right now. I know I've said this before, but this time I really mean it.

If I go home on December 19th I will follow all the rules at home, school, and all probation terms that you give me. If I'm on house arrest, I will be at home all the time. Every time the house arrest officer calls or comes over I will always be there. I would really appreciate that. I want to be home for the holidays.

If I keep on this "bad road" I will be in prison soon. So I want to change right now and be normal the rest of my life. I want to be a vet and on this path I will be nothing. So if I change right now, I might be able to complete my goal, which is to be a vet and take care of animals. I can be wealthy and support my mom if I quit doing things that are against the law.

I can have all the animals I want when I get older and have a big piece of land, but if I keep stealing, getting high, and not going to school, I won't have anything except a cardboard box *and be living on the streets. I really want to complete my goal and not mess up anymore.*

I have to stop hanging out with the bad friends and have a chance to make new ones. But in detention I can't do anything.

The reasons I want to change now is because I finally realized that it doesn't make me feel cool to go out and steal people's stuff, or come home high and no one catching me. It doesn't make me cool to be in detention for stealing or smoking pot.

If you let me go home for one month and don't see any changes, I will gladly come back. I say that because I believe I'll stay straight. Forever.

Sincerely,
Philip

I was glad to read that Philip was thinking about his future while in jail and was making positive plans. However, I had heard some of this from him before and I thought he needed additional time to think about his behavior. I didn't release him early or move up his hearing to an earlier date.

Throughout this period, Philip participated in counseling and anger management classes. Progress was slow but noticeable. Each time he was locked up, Philip claimed that all he wanted was to go home to take care of his pets. His psychiatrist described him as a young man who wanted to be independent, but who didn't know how to achieve it in positive ways. Family and friends were having a negative influence on his behavior.

In an attempt to have a fresh start away from his neighborhood, Philip moved to his grandparents' house, but he ran away after three weeks and returned to his mother's home.

PHILIP TODAY

Philip is now 15, living with his mother, and going to school. He has behaved himself and was returned to regular probation. He has ambitious goals. As stated in his letter, he wants to become a veterinarian. He takes care of his birds, chickens, ducks, and a snake. He knows if he makes the effort, he can become Dr. Philip. I plan to hand out his clinic's cards when the time comes.

FINAL THOUGHTS

Write down or discuss your thoughts:
- Were you surprised that Philip continued to get into trouble? Why or why not?
- Would you have done anything different in dealing with Philip as he returned to court each time?
- Would a harsher penalty for spitting at his mother have made a difference? Why or why not?
- Philip's mother introduced him to marijuana at age 10. Should she

be held responsible in some way for his behavior? If so, how? If not, why not?
- What should the court do if Philip shoplifts or uses marijuana again?
- What do you do when you get upset with one of your parents? Have you ever hit your mom or dad out of anger or frustration? Or cursed at them? How did that make you feel?
- Have you learned other ways to deal with anger—ways that you can pass on to your brothers and sisters? Do you have a plan for cooling off? (Some kids work out an agreement with their parents that when they are about to lose control, they have a code word that allows them to leave the house for a "safe place"—a neighbor, grandparent's home, or the backyard.)

Did You Know?

- Marijuana is the most widely used illegal drug. A 2003 study reported that 40 percent of teens say they've tried it at some point, including almost a half-million kids between 9 and 12 years old (Partnership for a Drug-Free America).

• A 2002 survey of 1,000 students found that it was easier to get marijuana than cigarettes or beer. Twenty-seven percent reported that they could get marijuana in an hour or less (National Center on Addiction and Substance Abuse, Columbia University).

RONALD*, 16

caught with beer and wine in a car

[* Ronald's name has been changed to protect his family's privacy.]

RONALD'S BACKGROUND LEADING UP TO THE CRIME

Ronald lives with his mother, a brother, and two younger sisters. His father died when he was a baby. When Ronald attends school he does well and is not a discipline problem. He's not involved in a gang and doesn't get into trouble either on or off the school grounds. He occasionally helps his older brother in his landscaping business. Ronald enjoys going to parties and likes to dance.

When he's 14, Ronald and two friends are stopped and questioned by the police because they're in an area where a truck had been broken into. He admits that they had joked earlier that day about taking a stereo from a car, but denies any involvement in the incident. Witnesses are unable to identify any of the suspects. No charges are filed.

Two months later, Ronald is ticketed for missing school. He admits the truancy and agrees to attend a few counseling sessions and complete 16 community service hours. He attends the counseling, but fails to do the community service. No further action is taken.

When Ronald is 15, he misses more school and is formally charged with truancy. This time he is placed on probation and ordered to complete 20 community service hours and attend a truancy-prevention class. But he continues to follow his own rules, doesn't do the assigned hours, and misses appointments with his probation officer. He is scheduled to appear in court on the probation violation.

RONALD'S CRIME: POSSESSION OF ALCOHOL

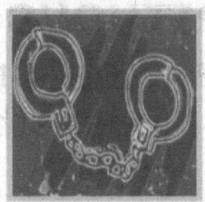

Before his court appearance, Ronald is out past midnight on a Sunday night in July with three friends. The police stop the car they're in because it has no license plate light. All four kids give the police their names and ages (15 and 16). The officers smell alcohol coming from the car and notice that the driver's eyes are red and watery. They are each tested at the scene and Ronald's breath test shows an alcohol concentration of .13, which is an illegal level. Beer and wine are found in the car. Ronald is arrested and taken to jail. He admits drinking and is charged with alcohol possession. He remains in jail awaiting sentencing.

Legal Definition of Possession of Alcohol

> It is unlawful for a person who is under the legal drinking age of 21 to **POSSESS, CONSUME, PURCHASE, OR SELL SPIRITUOUS LIQUOR.** This provision does not prohibit minors from working under the supervision of an adult in grocery stores, where the minor may package or carry out spirituous liquor in unbroken packages for the convenience of the customer.

YOUR CONCERNS AS A JUDGE

Before you is a teen who presents himself as a well-mannered, respectful young man. But he lacks motivation and has no interest in either school or working. He pays no attention to his mother or older brother, and does whatever he pleases.

Although Ronald wasn't charged with breaking into the truck, he admits being in the area at the time of the incident. You also know that he was given a chance last year to avoid going to court for truancy by doing 20 hours of community service, but he never did the work. In addition to the alcohol charge, he recently tested positive for marijuana.

You feel that no matter what you order Ronald to do, he'll agree to it in court and then do what he wants once the hearing is over. He is 16 and not doing anything with his time. You have a pretty good idea what he'll say to you at his sentencing, but you're not sure what you will say to him.

YOUR SENTENCING OPTIONS AS A JUDGE

A possession of alcohol offense can only be committed by someone under the age of 21. In most states it is considered a petty (or minor) offense and the penalties are usually a fine or community service hours. Some states allow the judge to place the juvenile on probation. An alcohol or drug awareness class is a common punishment. Jail time is uncommon, but in Ronald's case it's a possibility, given his past behavior.

Sentencing options available to you are:
- Jail time ranging from an additional week to a month, followed by one year of probation.
- Placement in a residential drug treatment program.
- Intensive probation, along with a fine, community service, an alcohol awareness class, and/or drug counseling.
- Regular probation with drug testing, drug abuse counseling, and an order to get back to school.
- No probation. Issue a warning to Ronald and close the case.
- Anything else?

QUESTIONS TO CONSIDER BEFORE SENTENCING RONALD

Write down or discuss your thoughts:
- Ronald has been involved in truancy, alcohol and drug abuse, and a possible theft. What behavior worries you the most? Why?
- Are you worried that Ronald will continue to get into more serious trouble? What can you do to try to prevent that?
- Ronald is an unmotivated teen who doesn't seem to care about following the rules. Do you simply lecture him and close the case? Or do you get tough with him? How are you going to get his attention?
- Since Ronald always violates probation, is there any point in giving him additional probation?

Should jail be tried instead? Or would jail possibly do more harm than good?
- How would you deal with Ronald's alcohol and marijuana use?
- Although Ronald's mother is caring and wants what is best for her son, she is unable to control him. Should you try to help Ronald's mother? How?

YOU BE THE JUDGE

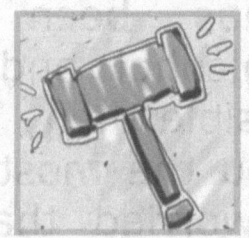

Complete this sentence:
Based on the information available to me, Ronald's sentence should be...

WHAT ACTUALLY HAPPENED

By the time Ronald came back to court for sentencing, he had already spent 18 days in jail. He appeared wearing a red shirt that told me he was

following all of the rules while locked up. (Red is the highest level inmates can achieve.) I decided to see if Ronald could once again try to follow through on all of his promises. I granted him time-served (meaning he was given credit for 18 days he just spent in jail) and sent him home on probation with the following terms:
- He was to take a drug test every week.
- Attend substance abuse counseling.
- Get back to school.

Based on his past behavior, I was worried Ronald wouldn't do what he promised. On the other hand, there eventually comes a time when most juveniles turn things around. Maybe this was Ronald's time.

YOUR RESPONSE TO THE JUDGE'S DECISION

Write down or discuss your thoughts:
- Are you surprised by the judge's sentence? Why or why not?
- Was it harder or easier on Ronald than your sentence? In what ways?
- What part of the judge's sentence do you agree with? What part do you disagree with? Why?
- Do you think Ronald will keep his promises this time? Why or why not?

RONALD AFTER SENTENCING

Ronald missed most of his drug abuse counseling sessions, as well as the weekly drug tests. When he did test, he was positive for marijuana and once for cocaine. This was a probation violation and he was sentenced to two weeks in jail.

Letter from Ronald While in Jail (age 17)

Dear Judge,

> *I am guilty of all my charges, but I am asking you to release me. I know this is not the first time I have violated my probation. I'm asking that you put me on intensive probation or home detention because of my family situation.*
>
> *I have been working for my brother doing landscape work. I am going to school on August 13 and I also have a girlfriend who is pregnant.*
>
> *I am sorry for the things that I have done and I promise to do better this time.*
> *Ronald*

When released, his probation terms remained the same, but I also ordered him to attend a five-day drug abuse program and a one-day prison tour as a warning.

Ronald did not appear for either program. His mother reported that he had run away. His probation officer went to the house and saw Ronald working on his car. Ronald took off running through the backyard and into a nearby alley. I had no choice but to issue a warrant for his arrest.

Soon after, Ronald was driving around with friends when one of them began shooting out the window. As he brought the gun back into the car it went off, striking Ronald in the back of the head. The passengers fled and Ronald's body wasn't found until hours later. His friend was charged with second-degree murder.

FINAL THOUGHTS

Write down or discuss your thoughts:
- What is your reaction to Ronald's death?
- Had Ronald been given more jail time after he was caught with alcohol, do you think things might have turned out differently? Why or why not?

- Could anything else have been done to help Ronald?
- What would you say to someone who is taking risky chances—whether it's drugs, questionable friends, weapons, or crime? Could you make a difference by speaking up? Why or why not?
- Have you faced similar temptations? How did you deal with them? What eventually happened?
- Is there a Ronald in your life, a friend you lost? How did that experience affect you?

Did You Know?

- Nine persons under age 19 are killed every day by firearms.
- In 1999, 3,385 children and teens were killed by gunfire in the United States—one child every three hours (Injury Facts 2002, National Safety Council).
- Over 70 percent of the total homicides, suicides, and gun-related deaths in the world's 26 richest countries occur among American children. More American kids die from

gunfire than from cancer, pneumonia, asthma, flu, and HIV/AIDS combined (Center for Disease Control and Prevention; Children's Defense Fund).

SAMANTHA, 14

unpaid cab fare and lying to police

SAMANTHA'S BACKGROUND LEADING UP TO THE CRIME

Raised by her father and stepmother, Samantha is the second of six children. She has had limited contact with her mother, who lives in another city and is reported to be an alcoholic. There have been reports to child protective services about abuse and neglect of Samantha and her siblings. However, workers did not find strong evidence of abuse and therefore no action was taken. Samantha's father has a history of drinking and domestic violence against Samantha's stepmother. In fact, he appeared drunk at one of Samantha's hearings.

Samantha starts running away when she's 12. She's usually gone for a few days, staying at the homes of friends. When she isn't on the run, she attends school and does well. She enjoys band and cheerleading, until she gets into a fight at school and is kicked off the squad.

SAMANTHA'S CRIME: THEFT AND FALSE REPORTING

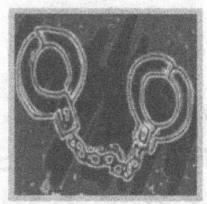

Samantha has run away from home again and decides to go to her older sister's home. She doesn't have any money, but calls for a cab to take her there. When they arrive, her sister isn't home. Samantha tells the cab driver that she can't pay the fare but will call her stepmother for help. She uses the driver's cell phone but is unable to reach her stepmom. The cab driver then calls the police.

Because she is on the run, Samantha is afraid of getting arrested and taken to jail, so she gives the police a false name and address and lies about her age. While she's talking with the police, her pager goes off. The police return the call and Samantha's sister answers. She is able to provide accurate information about Samantha, who is then arrested for theft of services (the cab fare) and providing false information to the police. When her stepmom is finally reached, she refuses to pick her up and Samantha is taken to jail.

Legal Definitions of Theft of Services and False Reporting

A person commits **THEFT OF SERVICES** if, without lawful authority, the person knowingly obtains services known to the person to be available only for payment, without paying; or controls property of another with the intent to deprive the other person of such property.

It is unlawful for a person to knowingly make to a law enforcement

> agency or representative, a **FALSE, FRAUDULENT, OR UNFOUNDED REPORT** or statement, or to knowingly misrepresent a fact for the purpose of interfering with the orderly operation of a law enforcement agency or misleading a peace officer.

YOUR CONCERNS AS A JUDGE

In Samantha's case, you are interested in why, at age 14, she is constantly running away from home and endangering herself by moving from place to place. The taxi incident and lying to the police officer are red flags that make you want to look further into her background. What is really going on with her father and stepmother? Although the child protective workers didn't find any evidence of abuse, that doesn't mean that abuse isn't taking place. And if Samantha's father has committed domestic violence and once came to court drunk, can you imagine what really goes on at home? Samantha's frequent running away may be her only escape from an abusive home, and this has to be investigated.

In preparing for Samantha's sentencing, you are given reports from Samantha's probation officer and a psychologist who interviewed her. The psychologist describes Samantha as a depressed and troubled teen because of her chaotic family background. She feels rejected by her parents because of their behavior toward her and toward each other. But Samantha understands she has problems and how they complicate her life.

Although not a threat to the community, Samantha's probation officer recommends that she not return home after being released from jail. Based on the number of times she has run away, it doesn't seem in her best interest to return home. Furthermore, her stepmother doesn't want her back. She tells the probation officer that

Samantha's behavior is affecting her younger brothers and sisters.

Samantha's case is about more than punishment. How should it be handled?

YOUR SENTENCING OPTIONS AS A JUDGE

If a person is found guilty of theft of services and false reporting, the usual penalty is a brief probation period and payment to the victim (in this case, the cabbie). Sometimes, a first offender is sentenced to a few days in jail. In Samantha's case, you also have to take into consideration her family and many other issues. You can consider the following options:
- A few days' jail time, with probation of three to six months.
- Placement in foster care temporarily, along with weekly

counseling, until you find out more about the family.
- Probation, with Samantha restricted to the house with an electronic ankle bracelet, drug testing, family counseling, and a requirement that her father go to Alcoholics Anonymous.
- Probation, along with individual and family counseling.
- No probation, but payment of the cab fare and a fine.
- Anything else?

Letter from Samantha While in Jail Awaiting Sentencing (age 14)

To Judge Jacobs:

My name is Samantha, and I have a few concerns regarding my release. If I am to be dismissed, I ask that you require counseling for me and my family. I have had two sessions with a therapist. She has had a positive influence on me. She has given me excellent advice and has taught me how to deal with my problems. I understand it may be an

> imposition to provide counseling and I apologize, but I would appreciate it very much. I completed a class in substance abuse. It also had a positive bearing on me and taught me many lessons.
> Thank you,
> Samantha

QUESTIONS TO CONSIDER BEFORE SENTENCING SAMANTHA

Write down or discuss your thoughts:
- Do you think Samantha should spend any more time in jail? Or would it be better for her to get probation? Why?
- In handling this case, how much do you take into account the family

situation? Was Samantha right to run away from home, given the fact that her father has a history of domestic violence and alcohol abuse? Did she have other options, instead of running away?
- Samantha didn't pay a cab fare after running away from an abusive home, and then lied to the police because she was afraid she'd be arrested. Do you view these as serious crimes? What's your definition of a serious crime?
- Should you put Samantha in foster care temporarily, while you find out more about what's going on in the family and what the family needs?
- What can you do to help Samantha and her family get along better? Would you order her father to stop drinking or to go to an alcohol treatment program? What about services for Samantha—does she need individual as well as family therapy?
- What is your reaction to Samantha's letter? How does it affect the sentence you give her?

YOU BE THE JUDGE

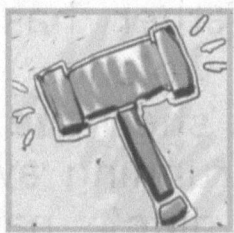

Complete this sentence:
Based on the information available to me, Samantha's sentence should be...

WHAT ACTUALLY HAPPENED

Samantha spent 27 days in jail before her sentencing hearing. I wasn't comfortable sending her home to her father and stepmother, where there might be abuse. I wanted further investigation done on the family. I couldn't take the risk of her being abused or neglected again, which would trigger another run from home. She also didn't need any more jail time. She was following the rules and wasn't a threat to anyone. In her letter, she said counseling in jail had helped her and wanted to continue counseling with her family.

I decided that the best thing to do was place her in a foster home and schedule another hearing in 30 days. I appointed a special guardian to investigate Samantha's family situation and make recommendations. I told Samantha to return to school and not run again, or she wouldn't get another chance at proving herself.

After a month in a foster home, Samantha and her parents came to court for the final hearing. Her father was sober and apologized for being drunk the last time he came to court. Based on the investigation of her family, I gave the following sentence to Samantha:

- I sent her home to her family and placed her on probation for an indefinite period, but told her she could earn her way off probation within a year if she followed her terms.
- Samantha would be tested for drugs by her probation officer.
- She was required to wear an electronic ankle bracelet so the court could monitor her whereabouts for the first 30 days. I didn't want

her to take off again. She agreed that the bracelet would help her stay put, but only time would tell.
- Samantha was required to participate in counseling with her family.
- In addition, her father had to attend Alcoholics Anonymous meetings.

> Many juvenile courts use an electronic bracelet to keep track of juveniles who aren't locked up. If the juvenile leaves the house, the bracelet triggers an alarm at a central office and the probation officer is notified. However, the young person is allowed to leave the house for school, counseling sessions, etc.

Samantha's father and stepmother agreed to accept her back home. They basically said they would do anything I ordered to be able to stay together. I was used to hearing all kinds of promises in the courtroom. But they looked and sounded sincere, so I thought it was worth trying.

YOUR RESPONSE TO THE JUDGE'S DECISION

Write down or discuss your thoughts:
- Are you surprised by the judge's sentence? Why or why not?
- Was it harder or easier on Samantha than your sentence? In what ways?
- What part of the judge's sentence do you agree with? What part do you disagree with? Why?
- What do you think of the judge's decision in allowing Samantha to go home at all? Are there any additional protections you would have put into place to assure Samantha's safety at home?
- Is anything missing from the judge's sentence? Why is it important?

- What worries, if any, do you have about Samantha's future?
- What should be done if Samantha runs away again?

SAMANTHA TODAY

Samantha did well for the next four months. She attended counseling with her father and stepmother. Then she began to miss school and her drug tests. She was 15 when she ran away again. A warrant was issued for her arrest, but she stayed on the run and avoided being arrested for the next year and a half.

During that period, she gave birth to a baby girl. Samantha was raising her daughter when she was found by the police and arrested for running away. To her credit, Samantha didn't commit any new crimes while she was gone from home. In fact, she called her probation officer several times, asking what she should do. She stayed away because she knew she'd be locked up and didn't want to give birth in jail.

Samantha was 16 now and locked up for the second time, this time for 17 days. I needed to keep her in custody so she wouldn't disappear again, until we could figure out the next step. Her baby was cared for by her father and stepmother while she was in jail. I had no concerns about her parents caring for the baby, because they had been on good behavior since Samantha's earlier arrest.

Once again, I had to decide what was best for her. Samantha was interviewed by a psychologist, who said that she appeared to be taking her responsibilities as a parent seriously. Her parents came to court with the baby and Samantha greeted her child warmly. Her emotional reaction must have gotten the better of me, because I was willing to send her home and give her another chance at probation. I ordered her to resume random drug testing, take parenting classes arranged by her probation officer, and participate in individual counseling.

This time Samantha didn't run away. She earned an early release from probation just after her 17th birthday. Samantha is now 19 and raising her 3-year-old daughter. They recently moved into their own apartment. She has worked at a doctor's office and is currently a full-time research coordinator for a medical data company. When I interviewed her, Samantha proudly displayed pictures of her daughter. The child's father has supervised visits with the baby, since he's on adult probation for drug offenses.

About her experience in detention, Samantha stated that she was terrified, scared, and lonely. "Juvenile hall made me realize I didn't want to go to adult jail. My second time woke me up."

FINAL THOUGHTS

Write down or discuss your thoughts:

- Are you surprised how Samantha's life turned out? Why or why not?
- Since Samantha's father had a history of domestic violence and once came to court drunk, would you have allowed Samantha's baby to go home while she was in jail, or would you have put the baby into foster care until Samantha came out of jail? Would you have put Samantha in jail at all?
- A juvenile court has no criminal control over adults, but what would you like to see happen to parents like Samantha's father and stepmother, who are suspected of abusing or neglecting their children? If there's no evidence, is there anything you can do?
- Samantha didn't think twice about taking a cab without having any money. In your opinion, is what she did really stealing? After all, what did she take—a little time and gasoline? Some people have the Robin Hood philosophy—it's okay to steal if the poor benefit. So stealing food from a local store or skipping out on a restaurant bill without

paying is all right. Nobody really loses and no one gets hurt. What do you think? Is stealing ever right?
- Have you faced any of the issues in your life that Samantha has faced? How have you handled them (counseling, peer groups, chat rooms, talking with a best friend)?
- Do you have a friend who is experiencing any of these problems? What can you do to help him or her? Besides being a good listener, is there something else you could do to help?

SEAN, 16

a pipe bomb in a bedroom drawer

SEAN'S BACKGROUND LEADING UP TO THE CRIME

Sean lives alone with his father. His parents divorced when he was 8. Sean's father used to have an alcohol problem and he physically and emotionally abused Sean as a child. But the father has been sober since Sean was 10, and now both parents want what is best for their son and are active participants in his life. Sean is close with an older sister who doesn't live at home.

Sean has good attendance at high school. He plays volleyball and basketball and works part-time as a busboy at a pizza restaurant. His father says Sean is extremely obedient with only a few curfew violations.

SEAN'S CRIME: MISCONDUCT WITH A WEAPON

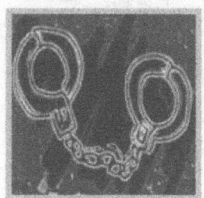

Sean is 16 when his father notices that his behavior is slipping at home and at school. He suspects Sean is using drugs and has him tested. The results indicate that Sean is smoking marijuana. When Sean's father searches his room for drugs, he finds a pipe bomb in Sean's dresser drawer.

A police bomb squad arrives and removes it from the home. The police question Sean and he admits that he had gotten the bomb from another kid. He doesn't say who gave it to him, but claims he planned on setting it off in a field someday to see what it was like. The bomb is big enough to blow up a small mailbox, but the police find no evidence that Sean was targeting people or property.

Sean's father feels the bomb is an isolated incident not likely to happen again. He is more concerned about his son's drug use and grounds Sean for three months. The case is sent to the prosecutor's office and Sean is charged with a weapons violation. He pleads guilty to a reduced charge of disorderly conduct with a dangerous weapon and is sent home to await sentencing before you.

Legal Definition of Misconduct with a Weapon

A person commits **MISCONDUCT WITH A WEAPON** by knowingly carrying a deadly weapon without a permit, except a pocket knife; possessing a deadly weapon if such person is a prohibited possessor (such as a convicted felon); defacing a deadly weapon; carrying a deadly weapon in a public place, after a reasonable request by the operator of the public place to remove the

> weapon; or by possessing such on school grounds or at a nuclear generating station.

YOUR CONCERNS AS A JUDGE

Sean's case is troubling. Here is a young man with great potential. He once had problems with his father, but now seems to have everything going for him. He likes school and does well in sports. His parents are involved with his life and his sister is always there for him. He has a job and plans for the future.

But now weapons and drugs have entered Sean's life. His father said the pipe bomb was a one-time incident. What if it's not? Can Sean be trusted to stay out of more trouble? Or is he literally a time bomb ready to go off?

What if he gets involved with more dangerous drugs and weapons? The police said Sean didn't intend to hurt anyone. But what about next time? On top of this, Sean doesn't understand why everyone is so upset with him.

You have to decide what is best for all concerned. You don't want to overreact and punish Sean too severely, but you also need to protect the community.

YOUR SENTENCING OPTIONS AS A JUDGE

Sometimes a young person has a good reason to have a knife, gun, or other type of weapon. He or she may like to hunt or practice target shooting. A pipe bomb in a teen's dresser is another story. Depending on the age of the offender and the parents' attitude about the incident, weapons charges typically result in probation with a fine and community service. A gun safety course might also be considered. A short stay in jail could be appropriate here, depending on Sean's attitude and behavior before sentencing. The other concern is Sean's drug use.

Sentencing options available to you are:
- A jail sentence ranging from a week to a month, followed by probation of up to one year.
- Participation in a high-impact drug abuse program conducted in jail for four days, with drug testing and a year of probation.
- Probation for up to one year, with a gun safety class, random drug tests, community service, and a fine.
- No probation, but a gun safety class and community service hours.
- Anything else?

QUESTIONS TO CONSIDER BEFORE SENTENCING SEAN

Write down or discuss your thoughts:
- Sean seems like a good kid who goes to school and usually stays out of trouble. He admits that he was going to explode the pipe bomb at some point, but in a field with no one around. Do you believe him?
- Does it matter that Sean won't say who gave him the pipe bomb? Do you believe another kid gave it to him?
- Does Sean need a dose of reality—a week or weekend in jail? Or is probation enough in this case?
- Sean's father grounded him for three months. Isn't that enough punishment? Why or why not?
- How would you deal with his drug use?

- Sean was physically and emotionally abused earlier in his life by his father. Could it have any connection with Sean having a pipe bomb? Should you try to find out if there are hidden problems at home contributing to Sean's behavior?

YOU BE THE JUDGE

Complete this sentence:
   Based on the information available to me, Sean's sentence should be...

WHAT ACTUALLY HAPPENED

Because of the seriousness of the charges, I wanted as much background information as possible about Sean. He was evaluated by a psychologist, who described him as having a good self-image. He was not impulsive and tended to think before he spoke. His probation officer reported that Sean was respectful at home and generally followed his curfew. He was popular among his peers and no gang involvement was suspected.

Based on the evidence and having met Sean in court, I tended to believe his story about getting the pipe bomb from another kid and wanting to set it off in a field out of curiosity. Nothing indicated that Sean had any intentions to harm people or property. His father had punished him by grounding him. I gave Sean the following sentence:

- I placed him on probation for a maximum of one year, with the possibility of early release if he fully complied with his terms, and ordered him to be tested for drugs once a week.
- He also had to attend a four-day substance abuse program in jail, which was, in effect, a short jail sentence.

I warned Sean that with just a few short months before his 18th birthday, it was time to wake up. Any future offenses would land him in the adult criminal system.

YOUR RESPONSE TO THE JUDGE'S DECISION

Write down or discuss your thoughts:
- Are you surprised by the judge's sentence? Why or why not?
- Was it harder or easier on Sean than your sentence? In what ways?
- What part of the judge's sentence do you agree with? What part do you disagree with? Why?
- Is there anything missing from Sean's sentence? Why is it important?
- What do you think will happen to Sean? Why?

SEAN AFTER SENTENCING

Sean started out by following all of his probation terms. He reported to the juvenile detention center and completed the four-day drug treatment program. He remained in school and kept working at the pizza restaurant.

But he also continued to use drugs. He violated probation three times, either testing positive for marijuana or not getting tested, as the rules required.

Sean was quickly approaching adulthood, where a drug offense could get him years, not weeks, in prison. I had to get across to him that he was endangering his future by his regular use of marijuana. I sentenced Sean, 17, to 27 days in jail. I hoped that nearly a month behind bars would give him the taste of an inmate's life and make him wake up.

Letter from Sean While in Jail (age 17)

Dear Judge Jacobs,

I am writing to you so you know how I feel and what I am going to do to get clean and stay clean. And what my objectives are when I get out. First I can say that 27 days in jail was the key. I had never been locked up before. I plan to get a job and stay active by playing golf or doing active sports. My big objective is to get my G.E.D. And go to a trade school for graphic printing. When I first came in here, like all detainees, I was a white shirt, but now I have been a red shirt for three days. I have lost only 2 points since I've been here and I have been following every direction given to me. But bottom line, I don't want to come back. The food is rotten, the sleeping arrangements suck ... uuhh, you know how it is. You're a judge, it's your job to know. Thanks for listening to what I have to say.

Your friend,
Sean

Sean was released to his father, who was willing to give him another chance. He stayed on probation and had to attend a one-day adult prison program designed to get the attention of older delinquents. He was also ordered to spend a day observing adult drug-court proceedings. I hoped both experiences would open Sean's eyes to what was in store for him if he continued on the same path.

Sean stayed on probation until he turned 18. Now he risked going to adult court if he committed another crime. Still, he continued to use drugs and steal money to buy drugs. He ended up spending a few months in adult jail and is now serving three years probation on drug charges and a stolen credit card charge.

SEAN TODAY

Sean lives in a halfway house for drug offenders and is staying clean and sober. He works full-time at a gas station/market. He rides his bike to work and has saved several thousand dollars, which he plans to put toward a car or a down payment on a house.

Sean wants to get off probation and get on with his life.

Looking back, Sean said that he "had to earn back my parents' trust and 'like'—they loved me, but didn't always like me. I've changed my way of thinking, from negative to positive. It's great to tell your father that you love him, and that he loves you, too."

FINAL THOUGHTS

Write down or discuss your thoughts:
- Were you surprised that Sean continued to do drugs and commit crimes? Why or why not?
- Do you think if Sean had gotten a harsher punishment for the pipe bomb incident—jail time instead of probation—he might have stayed out of trouble later on? Why or why not?
- What, in your view, is the most effective way to help kids get off

drugs? Jail them for a long time (maybe in adult jail)? Strict probation? Drug treatment programs? Counseling? A combination? Why?
- Why do some young people get involved with drugs? Why is it so hard to give them up?
- Sean attended several programs designed to "scare him straight"—such as visiting adult jails and observing adult drug court. Do you feel these "scared straight" programs have any impact on preventing crime by young people? Do you think you would learn anything from listening to a teen who has completed one of these programs? Why or why not?
- What do you think was at the heart of Sean's problems?

Did You Know?

In 2000, there were 37,600 juveniles arrested for possessing or carrying weapons. Of these, 90 percent were males and 33 percent were under age 15 (Office of Juvenile

Justice and Delinquency Prevention Statistical Briefing Book 2002).

STARLETT, 14

cutting school and violation of probation

STARLETT'S BACKGROUND LEADING UP TO THE CRIME

Starlett's parents separate when she's 14 and later divorce. She has a younger sister who lives with her father. Starlett moves back and forth between both parents. She thinks her father is too strict because he won't let her see her boyfriend, who is two years older. Her mother doesn't approve of the relationship either, since the boyfriend had a juvenile record. Both parents think Starlett may be using drugs but have no evidence, and they can't control Starlett.

Starlett goes to live with her grandmother for four months. Then she moves into her boyfriend's home with his parents, where she stays for almost a year. She keeps in touch with her parents, but refuses to return home to either one of them. Every time her parents or the police go to the boyfriend's house to find her, she isn't there.

At one point Starlett is picked up for running away and spends a night in jail before being released. At another point she's sent to a group home for a "cooling off" period of three weeks before returning home. When Starlett is 14, she starts missing school. She's required to attend a truancy-prevention class but doesn't show up. She's formally charged with truancy and placed on probation.

> Being placed on probation is not the end of the world. It simply means that an officer of the court (a probation officer) will be assigned to supervise you for a period of time. This could be from a few months to a year or longer, depending on your

behavior. The probation officer will be in touch with your parents, teachers, employer, and other adults to see how you're doing. The purpose of probation is to provide guidance and help when needed. Most kids placed on probation complete their term successfully and are released within a year.

STARLETT'S CRIME: VIOLATION OF PROBATION

Starlett is now in the 8th grade and by court order lives with her father, who had requested custody during the divorce proceedings with Starlett's mother. Her probation terms for truancy require that she attend school every day and the truancy-prevention class. But she claims that she and her father don't get along and that she doesn't like living there. Starlett runs away to a friend's home and stops going to school. As a result, her probation officer files a petition with the court charging Starlett with truancy and breaking her probation. She's put in jail for three weeks, awaiting sentencing.

Legal Definitions of Truancy and Violation of Probation

It is unlawful for any child between 6 and 16 years of age (each state sets its own age limits) to fail to attend school during the hours school is in session, unless the child is excused, instructed at home, exempted pursuant to statute, suspended, or expelled from school.

A person **VIOLATES HIS OR HER PROBATION** by knowingly breaking any of the written terms of probation ordered by the court.

A status offense is a violation of the law that only a minor can commit, for example, truancy, curfew, or running away.

YOUR CONCERNS AS A JUDGE

Seeing Starlett again, after placing her on probation earlier, is a concern but not a surprise. You are used to seeing teens like Starlett, who keep returning to court. The threat of probation or jail time doesn't magically change a lot of people.

Starlett is caught up in a pattern of running away from home, skipping school, and hanging out with questionable people. Her parents suspect Starlett of using drugs and can't control her, especially at night.

Although Starlett is before the court on seemingly harmless charges, this type of case is the toughest to decide. Some people say, "So what if a kid doesn't go to school? Or complete a truancy or behavior class? Who gets hurt? There are no victims. There is too much serious juvenile crime to have to spend time with minor offenders. Parents should handle these situations, not the courts."

It would be an easy decision to close this type of case. Simply take Starlett off probation, send her home, and hope you don't see her again on a more serious charge. The volume of cases in juvenile court is too high to justify time and resources on unruly kids who don't want to go to school or follow their probation terms. But is closing the case the right action to take?

A psychological evaluation shows that Starlett used to hang out with a gang, but never joined. She has been in a few fights and doesn't walk away from confrontations. She doesn't like school and doesn't think about her future. The psychologist recommends placement in a residential treatment facility, where she can get intensive therapy for anger control and family counseling.

Starlett's probation officer tells you something interesting in her report—she writes that Starlett is trying to make sense of her life and can be very successful in what she wants to do. But she needs help from her parents to make a positive change.

Her parents are concerned, but they're busy with their own lives. Can you do anything to bring them closer to Starlett? Or should you close the case, give her probation, and keep your fingers crossed?

YOUR SENTENCING OPTIONS AS A JUDGE

If you violate your probation and go back to court, the judge has a number of options. Depending on the seriousness of the violation, you may be given jail time or community service. Technical violations (as we see here with Starlett, missing school and leaving home) may not call for harsh penalties. A substantive violation occurs when someone commits another crime while on probation. This is more serious and has to be dealt with differently.

Your sentencing options for Starlett include:
- A weekend or two in jail, with probation up to one year, or longer, depending on Starlett's behavior.
- Placement at a residential treatment facility for six months, with ongoing individual and family counseling to deal with the issues behind Starlett's behavior.
- Probation, along with individual and family counseling, drug testing, community service, and banning Starlett from seeing her boyfriend for one year.
- A warning to Starlett and close the case.
- Anything else?

Letter from Starlett While in Jail Awaiting Sentencing (age 14)

Dear Judge Jacobs,
The first night that I was here I stayed up all night long and thought, "Is this what I want to

do for the rest of my life?" I then realized that this isn't me and this isn't who I remember being about one year ago.

I have a few things that I'd like to tell you. I had violated my probation by running away and missing a half an hour of my community service, so therefore I was put in jail. Since I've been in here, I have had lots of time to think things over, so this is what I have to say.

So, when I'm released, I am requesting that I have to take a urine analysis every other day, be put on house arrest for exactly one month, and that I have to visit with my probation officer every other week or every week. My plan for when I get out of here is to go to school every day. Right now I'm working on getting my 8th grade diploma so I can go to the right grade. I'm gonna graduate high school, then I'm gonna go to college and get my degree as a lawyer or as a nurse.

> *I also wanna volunteer at the hospital when I get out of here. Find new friends to hang out with.*
>
> *I made an oath to myself that I won't end up in here again. I also told myself that I'm a blind person putting my hands in God's hands, so therefore he can lead me in the right way. So, I wanna thank you for putting me here. It helped me realize who I really am and who I wanna be when I grow up.*
>
> *Sincerely,*
> *Starlett*

QUESTIONS TO CONSIDER BEFORE SENTENCING STARLETT

Write down or discuss your thoughts:

- Isn't Starlett's behavior the responsibility of her parents, not the courts? Should the court get involved in trying to discipline misbehaving teenagers? Or should it deal only with serious crimes?
- What can be done to help Starlett stay in one place and confront the issues that she's apparently running from? Jail would keep her in one place and counseling could be set up while she was there. But is that the answer—lock up every kid who doesn't like school or who won't live with one parent or the other?
- Starlett's boyfriend seems to be the main source of tension between herself and her parents. Should her parents be allowed to prevent her from seeing her boyfriend? Or is Starlett old enough to make her own decisions about who she spends time with? Is there anything you can do to ease that tension?
- Is the situation at home serious enough to have Scarlett put into a residential treatment program as the psychologist recommends?

- What would happen if you decided that this wasn't serious enough to take any more of the court's time—that other cases need your attention? Could you just lecture Starlett and her parents and send them on their way? Why or why not?
- What is your reaction to Starlett's letter? Does it affect the sentence you give her?

YOU BE THE JUDGE

Complete this sentence:
Based on the information available to me, Starlett's sentence should be...

WHAT ACTUALLY HAPPENED

When I saw Starlett at her sentencing, she had been in jail for three weeks. This was the first time she had ever been locked up. In her letter, she said she realized that lock-up wasn't what she wanted to do for the rest of her life. I believed her, and thought that the 21 days she served was enough to get her to settle down.

After talking with Starlett and her parents in court, I decided against a residential placement. Her parents seemed willing to work with her and participate in any programs that were set up to keep the family together. I was willing to give her a chance at home. I gave Starlett this sentence:
- Probation for up to a year, explaining to her that things could get better or worse—she could earn an early release or her probation could be extended, depending on her behavior.
- Individual and family counseling at home.
- Random drug tests.
- 20 hours of community service within the next month.
- I also restricted Starlett from any contact with her boyfriend for the next year. I wanted to remove the main source of tension with her

parents. I told her that she was still a minor and that her parents had the right to make some decisions for her, including who she hangs out with. If her parents wanted her to have contact with the boy, then fine. But that would have to wait until after she finished her probation, when her parents could decide. Until then, my order stood. Starlett didn't like it, but agreed to follow my order.

She said she would do everything required of her and I thought she might stay on track. I didn't want to see her again in court, and I told her so.

YOUR RESPONSE TO THE JUDGE'S DECISION

Write down or discuss your thoughts:

- Are you surprised by the judge's sentence? Why or why not?
- Was it harder or easier on Starlett than your sentence? In what ways?
- What part of the judge's sentence do you agree with? What part do you disagree with? Why?
- Would you have banned Starlett from seeing her boyfriend? Why or why not?
- Is there anything missing from the judge's decision? Why is it important?
- What do you think will happen to Starlett?

STARLETT TODAY

Starlett had her ups and downs over the next few years. She wasn't charged with any new crimes, but violated her probation a few times by running away and not completing her community service. She went back to jail three times for a total of nine days.

But then she started doing well on probation. All her drug tests have been clean and she expects to be off probation soon.

Starlett is now 17 and in high school. She lives with her mother and her mother's boyfriend. Starlett maintains contact with her father by phone and visits. She stayed away from her boyfriend as told and the relationship ended.

Starlett has worked part-time at a supermarket and at a doctor's office scheduling appointments. She is getting A's and B's in school and is thinking about becoming a nurse (on a maternity ward). She enjoys swimming, writing poetry, and hanging out with her friends.

When Starlett was in jail she was assigned a single cell and had no cellmate. She said that her cell was cold and she wanted to go home: "I didn't like being locked up in a little room." Her advice to others: "Trust me, don't do anything stupid. You don't want to be in jail, it's awful. Stay in school. It's the only way to make your dreams come true."

In Starlett's case, it may have taken two years to get results, but it was worth it. Where would Starlett be today if the court had simply dismissed her case and forgotten about her? In school? At home? Drug and gang free? Probably not.

In a few years, when Starlett assists a newborn baby and the parents at a hospital, she may think back to how the juvenile justice system helped her.

FINAL THOUGHTS

Write down or discuss your thoughts:
- Is there someone in your life who your parents don't want you to see? What do your parents say or do? How do you handle that? Have you tried to calmly discuss the situation?
- Are you able to put yourself in your parents' shoes to see their point of view? Would you like to reach a compromise with your parents?

What would it be? Do you think it's possible?
- Have you faced similar temptations in your life—thoughts of running away or skipping school? What happened? Would you do anything differently now?
- Looking back at Starlett's case, do you think parents may be just as effective in dealing with these issues as the police or courts? Does everything have to be handled formally in "the system"? Why or why not?
- Do you think there comes a time when the message finally sinks in and a young person makes some changes? Why do you think the message finally sinks in for some people and not others?

Did You Know?

There are approximately 500,000 juveniles on probation in the United States. The number one offense involves drug law violations, followed closely by property offenses, disturbing the peace, and personal offenses (assaults, etc.).

TANYA, 14

a stolen pregnancy test kit

TANYA'S BACKGROUND LEADING UP TO THE CRIME

Tanya's parents separate when she's 14. Her father moves to another state and Tanya lives with her mother. She stays in contact with her father by telephone and letters. Tanya has no brothers or sisters. She gets A's and B's in school and enjoys cheerleading.

In the 9th grade, Tanya starts cutting classes and eventually misses whole days of school. She begins hanging out with kids who turn her on to drugs. She has little respect for her mother, but doesn't want to move to her dad's home because she would miss her friends.

At 14, Tanya is caught in a vacant apartment with one of her friends and she's charged with criminal trespass. The next month she gets into an argument with her mother about going to school and Tanya breaks a window. She is charged with criminal damage. Soon after, Tanya and a girlfriend are out at 1:30A.m., and the police give them tickets for violating curfew.

When Tanya goes to court on these charges, she admits breaking the window and the other charges are dismissed. Tanya is placed on probation and required to go to school and attend counseling. She has already served 31 days in jail awaiting sentencing on these charges and you take that into consideration. Additional jail time does not seem necessary.

TANYA'S CRIME: SHOPLIFTING

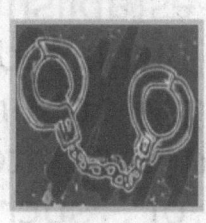

Late one night in a grocery store, Tanya is with another girl looking at pregnancy testers on a shelf. Security guards observe Tanya opening up the box, removing the tester, and putting it in her pants pocket. Tanya exits the store with her friend without paying for the item.

When the security guards approach Tanya, she immediately says that she did not steal anything and starts yelling, "Don't touch me, get away from me." A minor struggle takes place. The guards call the police and they arrest Tanya and question her. She admits to taking the pregnancy tester without paying for it. She says it was for a friend who she was concerned about. She is released to her mother to await sentencing.

Legal Definition of Shoplifting

A person commits **SHOPLIFTING** if, while in an establishment in which merchandise is displayed for sale, such person knowingly obtains such goods of another with the intent to deprive that person of such goods, by

> removing the goods without paying for them, or by concealing (hiding) the goods.

YOUR CONCERNS AS A JUDGE

Tanya is strong-willed, which can be a positive characteristic. However, in her case, a strong will has her headed in the wrong direction. She won't listen to her mother. But it doesn't make any difference whether Tanya lives with her father, because she can find trouble wherever she goes. She needs to take charge of her life, so she won't be in and out of jail. What can you do to help her stop making the wrong choices?

If you send her to jail, it will be her second time locked up. Will it make an impression this time? Or is there something else you could try instead of jail? She is not a danger to others, only to herself. Her probation officer reports that Tanya accepts responsibility for her acts. The psychologist who interviews Tanya tells you that she's depressed and in need of counseling. Does Tanya need counseling more than jail time? Or both?

Do you believe that she took the pregnancy tester for a friend? Or might have Tanya taken it for herself? She might be worried she's pregnant and wants to find out, while keeping it a secret from her mother. Or she could be telling the truth. When you released Tanya, you told her mother to see that Tanya gets medical attention in the event she is pregnant. You could have kept Tanya in jail before sentencing and made her take a pregnancy test, but these matters are often better left to the parents to handle.

Before her sentencing hearing, Tanya gets into more trouble. Her mother makes plans to send her to live with her father. The father sends Tanya's mother a check to cover some of the moving expenses. But then it looks like the plans have fallen through and Tanya won't be going after all. So she takes the check, changes her mother's name to hers, and attempts to cash it. Tanya gets caught and a forgery charge is filed against her. She admits what she did. You keep her in jail this time, while the final paperwork and transportation arrangements are made for her to live with her father. She will appear before you for sentencing on both the shoplifting and forgery charges.

What can you say to Tanya that might make a difference? What can you do so she doesn't get into worse trouble?

YOUR SENTENCING OPTIONS AS A JUDGE

Ordinarily, a shoplifting offense would result in some community service hours, along with a fine or payment to the store. Forgery is a felony and can possibly result in a jail sentence. At the very minimum, it results in probation time and payment to the victim for any monetary loss. In Tanya's case, she is already on probation for three minor offenses and now is facing sentencing on two new charges. Her behavior is getting worse and more severe options have to be considered.

Sentencing options available to you are:

- Jail time ranging from a month to two months, with continued probation for up to a year after release.
- Intensive probation (daily contact with a probation officer).
- Regular probation, with individual and family counseling.
- Additional counseling to the seven sessions Tanya already had during probation, and a day support program to keep her busy (day support monitors her activities throughout the day at school, and then provides an after-school program of recreation, counseling,

and tutoring if needed, followed by transportation home in the evening).
- Community service, a fine, and payment to the store.
- Anything else?

Letter from Tanya While in Jail Awaiting Sentencing (age 15)

Dear Judge Jacobs:

I was in your courtroom on March 27. You gave me a chance by putting me on home detention. Thank you for giving me that chance, and not putting me in jail right then and there.

But as you can see, I messed that up for myself. I have been in jail since April 16, and during that time I have realized a lot of things I never would have at home. I realized how much my mom really does care about me. She came to visit me every Monday and Thursday, and wrote me letters all the time. Despite all the stuff I put her through, she still stays by me and tells me that everything will be okay. And the best thing of all was when she comes to visit, we actually talk instead of fight. I liked the feeling of getting along with my mom instead of just fighting about everything.

Another thing I have realized is there are consequences for my actions, and if I keep doing what I am doing, then I'll keep going down this path. And I really don't want to be someone who goes in and out of detention centers. I want to be someone who makes something of herself in life.

In order to do that, though, I'll have to start following the rules and obeying my mother. When I go home I know I can do this, and continue to do this because I don't want to spend my teenage years in jail. I believe I am really a good kid, and can do better than that.

Sincerely,
Tanya

QUESTIONS TO CONSIDER BEFORE SENTENCING TANYA

Write down or discuss your thoughts:
- What should be the penalty this time, if any? What will help Tanya the most?
- Tanya says she stole the pregnancy tester to help a friend. Does this affect the sentence you give her? If so, how? If not, why not?
- Are you concerned Tanya is pregnant? Should the court do something to find out if she is, or counsel her about safe sex? Or is this Tanya's business?
- Should you consider just Tanya's criminal history (trespass, damage, curfew violation, and now shoplifting and forgery) or do you want to

know more about why she does these things?
- If Tanya goes home, what services do you have in mind for her and her mother?
- What is your reaction to Tanya's letter? Does it affect the sentence you give her? Why or why not?

YOU BE THE JUDGE

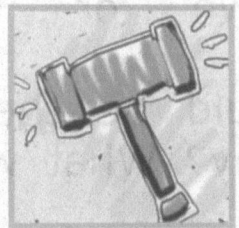

Complete this sentence:
With the information available to me, Tanya's sentence should be...

WHAT ACTUALLY HAPPENED

Tanya was escorted into my courtroom by a uniformed officer. She had spent 27 days in jail awaiting sentencing. Her mother appeared and sat next to Tanya. The mother told me that she had been visiting Tanya regularly over the past month and thought she saw a change in Tanya's attitude. She said she was willing to take her home, but would prefer that Tanya live with her father.

Tanya had talked with her father by phone several times while in jail. She agreed with my decision and said she would give it a try. I sentenced her to:
- One year of probation.
- Individual and family counseling to be set up by her probation officer while living with her father.

I told Tanya she would be assigned a new probation officer in her father's state. I didn't want her to think that she was free to do as she pleased, and told her that she could be quickly returned to my court if she violated her probation. Tanya never admitted that she took the pregnancy tester for herself, but she had told the psychologist who evaluated her that she had a boyfriend and was sexually active for the past year. I told Tanya and her mother that they should talk with each other about the responsibilities that go along with being sexually active—the risks involved, both physically and emotionally. I also told them that professional counseling was available if either of them requested it. Her mother was receptive to this, but Tanya was going to her father's. I asked her mother to pass along to him what we discussed, along with the need to exercise control over Tanya.

I told Tanya that a copy of her record would be sent to her new probation officer and juvenile court judge in her father's state. She was being given a chance at starting a new life at her father's, but her history couldn't be erased or ignored. I told her that the forgery incident was an example of how little she thought about consequences and acting responsibly.

If she followed her terms, I would gladly release Tanya from probation in one year. The 27 days she already served in jail was enough. I released her to her mother and she left for her father's house a few days later. I wished her the best and cautioned her to think long and hard before breaking the law again—she was running out of chances.

YOUR RESPONSE TO THE JUDGE'S DECISION

Write down or discuss your thoughts:
- Are you surprised by the judge's sentence? Why or why not?
- Was it harder or easier on Tanya than your sentence? In what ways?
- What part of the judge's sentence do you agree with? What part do you disagree with? Why?
- Is there anything missing from the judge's decision? Why is it important?
- How do you think Tanya will respond to living with her father? Do you think she'll change? Why or why not?

TANYA TODAY

After she moved into her father's home, Tanya returned to school and began individual and family counseling. There were a few conflicts at first (curfew, smoking, etc.) but, overall, Tanya settled into a daily routine. She was released from probation after 1 1/2 years of supervision. Four months after getting off probation, Tanya turned 17 and moved in with her 21-year-old boyfriend.

Tanya keeps in touch with both parents. She is a senior in high school, works part-time as a cashier, baby-sits on the weekend, and likes to read mysteries. Her plan is to finish school and become a teacher or a juvenile probation officer.

About being in jail, Tanya said, "I learned how much my family means to me. My father wrote and my mom visited every chance she could. I didn't think they cared, but I found out how much they did. I also learned that it wasn't how I wanted to spend my teenage years, or the rest of my life."

She continued: "I would tell kids today that it's not worth it, even being locked up for a few hours. It was the worst thing that ever happened to me. I was sick of being in trouble all the time. It's more fun to be safe and have a normal teenage life. When I moved to my father's, it was a big reality check—a new start. I messed up a bit at the beginning, but not as bad as before.

"My goals are to continue keeping myself out of trouble, and maybe when I get out of school I can help kids like me, like becoming a counselor or something like that."

FINAL THOUGHTS

Write down or discuss your thoughts:

- Are you surprised about how Tanya's life turned out? Why or why not?
- Have you had conflicts with parents or problems similar to Tanya's? What happened? How did the experience affect you?
- Shoplifting a pregnancy testing kit (or condoms) presents an interesting issue to the court. Should the crime be overlooked because the teen is worried about being pregnant or thinking of practicing safe sex? Or is it still a crime, no matter what was taken? Is this a time for punishment, for a lecture about abstinence and safe sex, or neither?
- Some judges would leave the sex education lecture to the parents. Unfortunately, too many parents depend on others (school, counselors, etc.) to discuss this topic with their kids. Do you believe that judges should talk to teens about sex education while they're in court? To all teens, or only to certain teens? If so, how do you decide who to have this talk with?

If the court doesn't do it, who will? Is it the court's business in the first place? Why or why not?

> ### Did You Know?
>
> • Actress Winona Ryder was convicted by a jury of shoplifting $5,500 in merchandise from a Beverly Hill's department store. The star of *Little Women, Mr. Deeds,* and *Girl Interrupted* was sentenced in 2002 to three years probation, 480 hours of community service, $10,000 in fines and restitution, and one day in jail (with credit for the day she was arrested and booked).
>
> • Hana Yaseem Ali (age 26), daughter of heavyweight boxer Muhammad Ali, was arrested in 2002 for attempted shoplifting (bedding) at a store in Canada. She agreed to complete a theft diversion program and no charges were filed.
>
> • Tennis star Jennifer Capriati was a teenager in 1993 when she was arrested for allegedly shoplifting a ring at a Florida mall. The charge was later dismissed.

Closing Arguments

You've just finished reading true stories about teens who got in trouble with the law. You've learned a lot about their family backgrounds, the crimes they committed, the punishments they received, and how their lives were changed. Take a few moments to think about your reactions to these stories. Write down or discuss your thoughts:

- What case or cases stood out for you in this book? Why?
- What surprised you the most? What did you learn?
- Many of the young people had difficult problems in their families—divorce, living with only one parent, poverty, living in crime or drug-ridden neighborhoods, etc. What was your reaction to their family life? How do you think it affected their behavior or the decisions they made?
- Have your feelings about the juvenile justice system or of crime by young people changed after

reading this book? If so how? If not, why not?
- Were most teens in this book treated fairly and helped by the system?
- What could be done to prevent or lessen crime by teens?
- What would you most like to change about the juvenile justice system?
- What would you like to know more about?
- Have you thought about being a social worker, probation officer, lawyer, or judge? Does the juvenile justice system appeal to you as a future career?

Resources

BOOKS/VIDEOS

Addiction: The High That Brings You Down by Miriam Smith McLaughlin (Berkeley Heights, NJ: Enslow Publishers Inc., 1997). Including discussions of both substance abuse and behavioral disorders, *Addiction* lists causes, characteristics, and results of uncontrolled, compulsive activities as well as places where teenage addicts can find help and support at school and in the community.

Alcohol video by Cambridge Educational (200 American Metro Blvd., Suite 124, Hamilton, NJ 08619; 1-800-257-5126). This video includes personal accounts of teens and comments from counselors regarding parental responsibilities.

Drugs and Sports by Peggy Parks (San Diego, CA: Reference Point Press, 2010). This book looks at the use of performance-enhancing and illicit drug use among athletes from all sides of the debate.

Fighting Invisible Tigers: Stress Management for Teens (Revised and Updated Third Edition) by Earl Hipp (Minneapolis: Free Spirit Publishing, 2008). Written for teens who are overwhelmed, frustrated, tired, or stressed out by the challenges in their lives, this book offers stress-management and life-management skills.

Gun Control edited by Helen Cothran (San Diego, CA: Greenhaven Press, 2002). Sociologists, activists, and others debate whether stricter gun control measures would reduce the number of school shootings and other gun-related problems.

How Long Does It Hurt: A Guide to Recovering from Incest and Sexual Abuse for Teenagers, Their Friends, and Their Families by Cynthia L. Mather (San Francisco: Jossey-Bass, 2004). This step-by-step guide speaks directly to victims of sexual abuse to help them overcome their feelings of isolation, confusion, and self-doubt.

In Love and In Danger: A Teen's Guide to Breaking Free of Abusive Relationships by Barrie Levy (New York:

Seal Press, 2006). This book includes facts about dating violence, tips for how to tell if your relationship is abusive, information on why dating abuse happens, and advice on what to do if you are being abused.

The Kids' Guide to Money: Earning It, Saving It, Spending It, Growing It, Sharing It by Steve Otfinoski (New York: Scholastic, 1996). This book explains to kids the fundamentals of how to thrive in the American economy. The author promotes the joys of work, finding a job or building a business, developing advertising as well as provides explanations of banks, budgets, careful consumerism, taxes, investments, and charitable donations.

The Kid's Guide to Service Projects: Over 500 Service Ideas for Young People Who Want to Make a Difference (Updated 2nd Edition) by Barbara A. Lewis (Minneapolis: Free Spirit Publishing, 2009). This guide shows how to make a difference, from simple projects to large-scale commitments, in several service areas including animals, the environment, crime fighting, hunger, literacy, and more.

Life Lists for Teens: Tips, Steps, Hints, and How-Tos for Growing Up, Getting Along, Learning, and Having Fun by Pamela Espeland (Minneapolis: Free Spirit Publishing, 2003). More than 200 self-help lists cover topics ranging from health, cyberspace, school success, personal safety, to friendship and fun.

Real Kids, Real Stories, Real Change: Courageous Actions Around the World by Garth Sundem (Minneapolis: Free Spirit Publishing, 2010). Thirty true stories about kids and teens from around the world who have overcome tremendous odds to make a difference.

Respect: A Girl's Guide to Getting Respect & Dealing When Your Line Is Crossed by Courtney Macavinta and Andrea Vander Pluym (Minneapolis: Free Spirit Publishing, 2005). Covers topics girls deal with daily, like body image, family, friends, the media, school, relationships, rumors, and more.

The Struggle to Be Strong: True Stories by Teens About Overcoming Tough Times edited by Al Desetta and Sybil Wolin (Minneapolis: Free Spirit Publishing, 2000). Thirty teens, in first-person stories, tell how they overcame major life obstacles using the seven resiliencies: insight, independence, relationships, initiative, creativity, humor, and morality.

Teenage Fathers by Karen Gravelle and Leslie Peterson Caputo (Lincoln, NE: iUniverse.com, 2000). Thirteen young men talk honestly and passionately about what it means to be a parent.

The Teenagers' Guide to School Outside the Box by Rebecca Greene (Minneapolis: Free Spirit Publishing, 2001). This book describes a world of possibilities, from study abroad to internships, apprenticeships, networking, job shadowing, service learning, university coursework, and independent study.

When Nothing Matters Anymore: A Survival Guide for Depressed Teens (Revised and Updated) by Bev Cobain (Minneapolis: Free Spirit Publishing, 2007). This book describes the causes and types of depression, and discusses different kinds of treatment, how they help, and how to stay healthy. Includes true stories from teens who have dealt with depression, survival tips, and resources.

Wise Highs: How to Thrill, Chill, & Get Away from It All Without Alcohol or Other Drugs by Alex J. Packer (Minneapolis: Free Spirit Publishing, 2006). This book offers safe, creative, natural ways to relieve stress, get a rush, and find peace, pleasure, excitement, and insight.

Your Pregnancy & Newborn Journey: A Guide for Pregnant Teens by Jeanne Warren Lindsay and Jean Brunelli (Buena Park, CA: Morning Glory Press, 2004). This comprehensive resource helps teenagers through every step of early motherhood. Also includes a chapter for teenage dads.

JOURNAL ARTICLES

"Drug Testing for Youthful Offenders on Parole: An Experimental Evaluation" by Rudy Haapanen and Lee Britton, 1 *Criminology and Public Policy* 217 (2002).

"Dusk 'Til Dawn: Children's Rights and the Effectiveness of Juvenile Curfew Ordinances" by Brian Privor, 79 *Boston University Law Review* 415 (1999).

"Criminal and Civil Parental Liability Statutes: Would They Have Saved the 15 Who Died at Columbine?" by Eric Paul Ebenstein, 7 *Cardozo Women's Law Journal* 1 (2000).

"From Adolescent 'Serious Offenders' to Adult Felon: A Predictive Study of Offense Progression" by Brent B. Benda, Robert F. Corwyn, and Nancy J. Toombs, 32 *Journal of Offender Rehabilitation* 79 (2001).

"Getting Tough on Crime: Juvenile Waiver and the Criminal Court" by Christina DeJong and Eve Schwitzer Merrill, 27 *Ohio Northern University Law Review* 175 (2001).

"Intervening with Youthful Substance Abusers: A Preliminary Analysis of a Juvenile Drug Court" by Brandon K. Applegate and Shannon Santana, 21 *Justice System Journal* 281 (2000).

"Juvenile Offenders in Criminal Court and Adult Prison: Legal, Psychological, and Behavioral Outcomes" by Richard E. Redding, 50 *Juvenile and Family Court Journal* 1 (1999).

"Killer Party: Proposing Civil Liability for Social Hosts Who Serve Alcohol to

Minors" by Matthew C. Houchens, 30 *John Marshall Law Review* 245 (1996).

"Manual to Combat Truancy" by the U.S. Department of Education, 1996. See www.ed.gov/pubs/Truancy

"Parental Liability for Youth Violence: The Contrast Between Moral Responsibilities and Legal Obligations" by Deborah A. Nicholas, 53 *Rutgers Law Review* 215 (2000).

"Pre-Offense Monitoring of Potential Juvenile Offenders: An Examination of the Los Angeles County Probation Department's Novel Solution to the Interrelated Problems of Truancy and (Juvenile) Crime" by Charles Edward Pell, 73 *Southern California Law Review* 879 (2000).

"Schools Can Test Students in Extracurricular Activities for Drug Use," Supreme Court Debates, September 2002, Volume 5, Number 6.

"Students or Serfs? Is Mandatory Community Service a Violation of the Thirteenth Amendment?" by Bradley H. Kreshek, 30 *Loyola University at Los Angeles Law Review* 809 (1997).

"The Sudden Popularity of Teen Courts" by Jeffrey A. Butts and Janeen

Buck, 41 *Judges' Journal* 29 (Winter 2002).

"Tenuous Borders: Girls Transferred to Adult Court" by Emily Gaarder and Joanne Belknap, 40 *Criminology* 481 (2002).

"Understanding Recreation and Sport as a Rehabilitative Tool Within Juvenile Justice Programs" by D.J. Williams, William B. Strean, and Enrique Garcia Bengoechea, 53 *Juvenile and Family Court Journal* 31 (2002).

"Where Are the Parents? Parental Criminal Responsibility for the Acts of Children" by Lisa Lockwood, 30 *Golden Gate University Law Review* 497 (2000).

CRISIS HOTLINES

Bureau for At-Risk Youth

1-800-99-YOUTH (1-800-999-6884)
www.at-risk.com

Help and advice for raising happy, healthy children.

Center for Substance Abuse Treatment

1-800-662-HELP (1-800-662-4357)
For counseling and referrals in emergencies.

Covenant House Nineline

1-800-999-9999
www.covenanthouse.org
Immediate help in crisis situations. This Christian-based organization provides free material and emotional support for runaways.

National Association for Shoplifting Prevention

1-800-848-9595
Call to request printed materials or CDs for a home-study program.

National Runaway Switchboard

1-800-621-4000
A referral service for youth in personal crisis. All calls are confidential.

National Sexual Assault Hotline

1-800-656-HOPE (1-800-656-4673)
Sponsored by RAINN (see section entitled "RAINN (Rape, Abuse & Incest National Network)" for more information), calls are routed to a rape crisis center in the caller's area code.

Teen Line

1-800-852-8336
teenlineonline.org
A confidential peer-mediated helpline open to any discussion topic from 6p.m. to 10p.m. (PDT).

ORGANIZATIONS

Al-Anon and Alateen

Al-Anon Family Group Headquarters, Inc.
1600 Corporate Landing Parkway
Virginia Beach, VA 23454-5617
(757) 563-1600
www.al-anon.alateen.org

Al-Anon is a worldwide organization that provides support to families and friends of alcoholics; Alateen is for younger family members who are affected by someone else's drinking. Request their free packet of teen materials.

Alcoholics Anonymous World Services, Inc.

P.O. Box 459
New York, NY 10163
(212) 870-3400
www.aa.org

Alcoholics Anonymous is worldwide with meetings in almost every community. Membership is open to anyone who wants to do something about his or her drinking problem. Telephone numbers for Alcoholics Anonymous are often listed in local telephone directories.

Cocaine Anonymous World Services

P.O. Box 492000
Los Angeles, CA 90049-8000

(310) 559-5833
www.ca.org

Cocaine Anonymous is a fellowship of men and women who share their experience, strength, and hope with each other that they may solve their common problem and help others to recover from their addictions.

D.A.R.E. (Drug Abuse Resistance Education)

1-800-223-3273
www.dare-america.com

Information on D.A.R.E.'s anti-drug, anti-violence message for kids, parents, educators, and D.A.R.E. officers.

MADD (Mothers Against Drunk Driving)

MADD National Office
511 East John Carpenter Freeway, Suite 700
Irving, TX 75062
1-800-438-MADD (1-800-438-6233)
www.madd.org

MADD's mission is to stop drunk driving, support the victims of this violent crime, and prevent underage drinking.

Marijuana Anonymous World Services

P.O. Box 2912
Van Nuys, CA 91404
1-800-766-6779
www.marijuana-anonymous.org

Marijuana Anonymous is a fellowship of men and women who share their experience, strength, and hope with each other so that they may help others recover from marijuana addiction. Check out their Web site for information and local referrals.

Narcotics Anonymous

World Service Office
P.O. Box 9999
Van Nuys, California 91409
(818) 773-9999
www.wsoinc.com

Narcotics Anonymous is an international, community-based association of recovering drug addicts with more than 43,900 weekly meetings in over 127 countries worldwide.

National Clearinghouse for Alcohol and Drug Information

1-800-SAY-NO-TO (1-800-729-6686)
www.ncadi.samhsa.gov

An organization of the federal government providing free information on substance abuse. National Clearinghouse for Alcohol and Drug Information (NCADI) is the nation's one-stop resource for free information about substance abuse prevention and addiction treatment.

RAINN (Rape, Abuse & Incest National Network)

2000 L Street NW, Suite 406
Washington, DC 20036
(202) 544-1034
www.rainn.org

RAINN is the nation's largest anti-sexual assault organization. It created and operates the National

Sexual Assault Hotline (1-800-656-HOPE); publicizes the hotline's free, confidential services; educates the public about sexual assault; and leads national efforts to improve services to victims and ensure that rapists are brought to justice.

SADD (Students Against Destructive Decisions)

SADD National
255 Main Street
Marlborough, MA 01752
1-877-723-3462
www.sadd.org

Students helping students make positive decisions about challenges in their everyday lives. Consider signing the SADD "Contract for Life" with your parents. To get your own signable copy, contact SADD.

WEB SITES

Canadian Legal FAQs

www.law-faqs.org

Questions and answers about shoplifting and other crimes in Canada.

Mental Help Net

www.mentalhelp.net
Tons of links to sites with self-help information on a wide variety of health issues including alcohol and drug abuse.

National Institute on Drug Abuse for Teens

teens.drugabuse.gov
This site, sponsored by the National Institute on Drug Abuse, includes stories from real recovering teens, interactive facts on drugs and drug addiction, and "Ask Dr. Nida."

R.A.D. Systems (Rape Aggression Defense)

www.rad-systems.com
Taught by nationally certified instructors, these practical self-defense classes take place throughout the United States at no to minimal cost.

Sex, Etc.

www.sexetc.org

An award-winning site run by and for teens by Rutgers University's Answer, it offers information about teen sexual health issues geared toward young adults.

TeenCentral.net

www.teencentral.net

This anonymous help line Web site by KidsPeace is for teens, by teens. Developed by experts in teen counseling and psychology, professionally monitored, and password-protected, it's a safe cyberspace where teens can work out their issues.

Women's Sports Found

www.womenssportsfoundation.org

This site encourages girls and parents to educate themselves about and act against gender discrimination in sports. It champions female athleticism and provides links on federal Title IX rules, coaching, and parental involvement.

About the Author

Thomas A. Jacobs, J.D., was an Arizona Attorney General from 1972–1985, where he practiced criminal and child welfare law. He was appointed to the Maricopa County Superior Court in 1985, where he served as a judge pro tem and commissioner in the juvenile and family courts until his retirement in 2008. He also taught juvenile law for 10 years as an adjunct professor at the Arizona State University School of Social Work. He continues to write for teens, lawyers, and judges.

Visit his Web site, Askthejudge.info, for free interactive educational tools that provide current information regarding laws, court decisions, and national news affecting teens. It's the only site of its kind to provide legal questions and answers for teens and parents with the unique ability to interact with Judge Jacobs and other teens.

Other Great Books from Free Spirit

Teen Cyberbullying Investigated

Where Do Your Rights End and Consequences Begin?
by Thomas A. Jacobs, J.D.
This collection of landmark court cases involves teens and charges of cyberbullying and cyberharassment. Each chapter features a seminal cyberbullying case and resulting decision, asks readers whether they agree with the decision, and urges them to think about how the decision affects their lives. For ages 12 & up.

Teens Take It to Court

Young People Who Challenged the Law—and Changed Your Life
(Revised and Updated Edition)
by Thomas A. Jacobs, J.D.

Can teens go all the way to the Supreme Court—and win? This book describes precedent-setting cases that reveal the power of social action and proves that even teens can change the law. Recommended for all young people, teachers (especially social studies and sociology), and youth workers in the legal system. For ages 12 & up.

What Are My Rights?

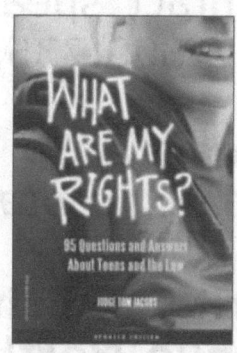

95 Questions and Answers About Teens and the Law
(Revised and Updated Edition)
by Thomas A. Jacobs, J.D.

Teens need to know about the laws that affect them to make informed decisions about what they should and shouldn't do. This fascinating book helps teens understand the law, recognize their responsibilities, and appreciate their rights. For ages 12 & up.

Interested in purchasing multiple quantities?
Contact edsales@freespirit.com or call 1.800.735.7323 and ask for Education Sales.
Many Free Spirit authors are available for speaking

engagements, workshops, and keynotes. Contact speakers@freespirit.com or call 1.800.735.7323.

To place an order, or to request a free catalog, contact:

**Free Spirit Publishing Inc.
217 Fifth Avenue North • Suite 200
• Minneapolis, MN 55401-1299
toll-free 800.735.7323 • local 612.338.2068 • fax 612.337.5050**
help4kids@freespirit.com • www.freespirit.com

Index

A

Adjusted, *135*
Adult criminal system,
  described, *98*
  juveniles prosecuted in, *98, 102, 109, 114*
  Kids visit prison programs in, *86, 93*
  penalties in, *255, 329, 331*
  probation in, *102*
Aggravated assault, *119, 275*
Alcohol,
  abuse of, *248*
  availability and, *25, 31*
  awareness classes for, *240*
  driving under influence of, *248*
  experimenting with, *86, 170*
  extent of juvenile use of, *151*
  legal drinking age, *238*
  at parties, *236, 238, 240*
  possession or consumption of, legal definition of, *238, 291*
  sentencing options for, *240, 242, 292*
Ali, Hana Yaseem, *371*
Assault,
  degrees of, *119, 275*
  legal definition of, *155, 273*
  restitution for, *157*
  sentencing options for, *82, 84, 121, 123, 157, 275*
Auto theft,
  arrests for, *268*

legal definition of, *98, 252*
sentencing options for, *102, 255, 257*

B
Bullying, *39*
Burglary,
  described, *22, 175*
  legal definition of, *80, 172, 194*
  restitution for unrecovered items, *179, 181*
  sentencing options for, *82, 84, 175, 177*

C
Capriati, Jennifer, *371*
Cocaine, *151*
Community service,
  as diversion, *2*
  as job training, *181*
  types of, *183, 232*
Consequences, *135*
Counseling, *93*
Credit card theft,
  legal definition of, *100*
  sentencing options for, *102*
Crimes,
  felonies,
    forgery, *360*
    sentencing options for, *102*
  minimum chargeable age for, *273*
  misdemeanors, *102*
Criminal damage, *117*

D
Day support programs, *177, 181*
Deaths, *248, 300*
Deferred jail time, *142*
Disorderly conduct, *90, 117*
Diversion,
  described, *4*
  programs, *2, 207, 210*
Domestic violence,

exposure of juveniles to, *57*
legal definition of, *44*
sentencing options for, *48*
Drinking,
See Alcohol, abuse of,
Driving under influence, *248*
Dropouts, *219*
Drug abuse,
See Illegal drugs,
Drunk driving, *248*

E
Electronic ankle bracelets, *68, 313*
Employment, *219*

F
False reporting,
described, *96*
legal definition of, *305*
sentencing options for, *307, 309*
Felonies,
forgery, *360*
sentencing options for, *102*
Female juveniles,
abuse of alcohol by, *248*
arrests for auto theft by, *268*
as domestic violence victims, *57*
as runaways, *75, 168*
violence by, *132*
weapons possession by, *151, 334*
Firearms, *300*
See also Weapons,
Fireworks, *93*
First-time offenders,
diversions for, *4*
Mock Lock Ups, *86*
programs for, *20*
sentencing and, *175*
Food supplements, *203*

Forgery,
  legal definition of, *100*
  sentencing options for, *102, 360, 362*

G
Gangs, *20, 135, 140, 151*
Good behavior, *131*
Guns, *18, 300*
  See also Weapons,

H
High impact programs,
  described, *20*
  'Kids visit prison' programs, *86, 93*
  'Mock Lock Ups', *84, 86*

I
Illegal drugs,
  abuse of,
    after sentencing, *68*
    truancy and, *59*
  adult criminal system penalties for, *329, 331*
  availability of,
    abuse and, *25, 31*
    in schools, *39, 151*
  experimenting with, *86, 170*
  medications as, *203*
  paraphernalia for, legal definition of possession of, *155*
  possession of,
    legal definition of, *138*
    sentencing options for, *140, 142*
  during probation, *353*
  treatment programs, lack of sufficient, *31, 37*
  zero tolerance in schools, *203*
  See also Marijuana,

Incarceration,
  in adult jails, *98*
  deferred, *142*
  effect of, *57, 70, 90, 183, 185, 218, 331*
  good behavior during, *131*
  minimum age for, *273*
  programs during, *20, 33*
  before sentencing, *121, 123, 144*
Indictments,
  See Charges,
Intensive probation, *9, 33, 142, 191*
Intimidation,
  ability to carry through, *7, 9, 11, 13*
  legal definition of, *4*
  sentencing options for, *7, 9*

J

Jails,
  See Incarceration,
Joyriding, *77, 252*
Judges,
  limitations placed upon, *33*
  mediation agreements and, *44*
  See also High impact programs,
Juvenile justice system,
  funding of programs, *279*
  jurisdiction of, *98*
  rarity of repeat offenders in, *267*
Juveniles,
  arrested for rape, *168*
  number living in poverty, *187*
  prosecuted as adults, *98, 102, 109, 114*
  rights of, *18, 224*
  See also Female juveniles; Male juveniles,

K

Kids visit prison programs, *86, 93*

L

Lawyers,
See Attorneys,
'Life Sentence' (class), *68*

M

Male juveniles,
abuse of alcohol by, *248*
arrests for auto theft by, *268*
as domestic violence victims, *57*
robberies by, *39*
weapons possession by, *334*

Marijuana,
availability of, *75, 286*
extent of use of, *286*
possession of,
legal definition of, *61*
sentencing options for, *64*
use by juveniles, *151*

Medications, *203*

Misconduct with weapons, *323*

Misdemeanors, *102*

Mock Lock Ups, *84, 86*

N

Narcotics,
See Illegal drugs,

P

Peer groups, *194*
Penalties, *135*
Petitions,
See Charges,
Plea bargains or agreements,
described, *22*
effects of, *196*
Pleas,
changing, *225*
sentencing and, *44*
trials and, *44*

Possession of alcohol,
  legal definition of, *238, 291*
  sentencing options for, *240, 242, 292*
Possession of drug paraphernalia, legal definition of, *155*
Possession of illegal drugs,
  legal definition of, *138*
  sentencing options for, *140, 142*
Possession of marijuana,
  legal definition of, *61*
  sentencing options for, *64*
Possession of weapons, *151, 334*
Prescription drugs, *203*
Probation,
  in adult criminal system, *102*
  described, *338*
  intensive, *9, 33, 35, 142, 144, 191*
  Kids visit prison programs and, *93*
  number of juveniles on, *353*
  standard terms of, *189*
  violations of, *61, 68, 183*
  legal definition of, *338*
  sentencing options for, *343*
  types of, *343, 353*
Probation officers, *82*
Programs,
  day support, *177, 181*
  diversion, *2, 207, 210*
  drug treatment, *31, 37*
  for first-time offenders, *20*
  funding of, *279*
  high-impact,
    described, *20*

'Kids visit prison', 86, 93
'Mock Lock Ups', 84, 86
residential,
   described, 166
   lack of sufficient, 263
   for runaways, 166, 279
   short-term in juvenile jails, 33
Programs at, 20, 33
Property crimes, 175
Prosecutors, 4

R

Rape, 160, 168
Repeat offenders,
   diversions and, 4
   programs undergone by, 96, 100
   rarity in juvenile justice system of, 267
   sentencing of, 175, 177, 362
   for truancy, 288
Residential treatment programs or facilities,
   lack of sufficient, 263
   for runaways, 166
Restitution,
   for assault, 157
   for burglary, 179, 181
   for damaged property, 259, 261
   for forgery, 360, 362
   for theft of services, 307
Robbery,
   described, 22
   number of juveniles arrested for, 39
   sentencing options for, 26
Robin Hood philosophy, 318
Runaways,
   arrests for, 75, 168
   programs for, 166, 279
Ryder, Winona, 371

S

Scared straight programs,
  See High impact programs,
School interference, legal definition of, *4*
Schools,
  discipline problems in, *18*
  dropouts from, *219*
  gangs in, *151*
  illegal drugs in,
    availability of, *39, 151*
    zero tolerance and, *203*
  importance of academic record in, *11*
  salaries and education level, *219*
  suspension from, *203*
  truancy from,
    drug abuse and, *59*
  legal definition of, *207, 338*
  repeat offenders, *288*
  seriousness of, *341*
  violence in, *39*
  weapons in, *18, 151*
Sentencing,
  drug abuse after, *68*
  first-time offenders, *175*
  incarceration before, *121, 123, 144*
  pleas and, *44*
  repeat offenders, *175, 177*
  of repeat offenders, *362*
  scheduling hearings for, *224*
Sentencing options,
  for assault, *82, 84, 121, 123, 157, 275*
  for auto theft, *102, 255, 257*
  for burglary, *82, 84, 175, 177*

for credit card theft, *102*
for domestic violence, *48*
for false reporting, *307, 309*
for felonies, *102*
for forgery, *102, 360, 362*
for illegal drugs possession, *140, 142*
for marijuana possession, *64*
for probation violations, *343*
for robbery, *26*
for shoplifting, *225, 360, 362*
for theft, *196*
for theft of services, *307, 309*
for threatening, *7, 9*
for trespass, *175, 177*
for truancy, *64, 210, 212*
for weapons charges, *325*

Services, theft of,
    described, *250*
    legal definition of, *305*
    sentencing options for, *307, 309*
Shirt system, *131*
Shoplifting,
    examples of, *233*
    by famous people, *371*
    legal definition of, *224, 357*
    number of incidents of, *233*
    sentencing options for, *225, 360, 362*
Status offenses, *338*

T

Theft,
    auto,
        arrests for, *268*
        legal definition of, *98*
        sentencing options for, *102, 255, 257*

credit card, *100, 102*
described, *22*
legal definition of, *25, 194*
sentencing options for, *196*
of services,
  described, *250*
  legal definition of, *305*
  sentencing options for, *307, 309*
See also Burglary,
Threatening,
ability to carry through, *7, 9, 11, 13*
legal definition of, *4*
sentencing options for, *7, 9*
'Throw aways', *168*
Tickets,
  See Citations,
Tobacco, use by juveniles, *151*
Trespass, *175, 177*
Trials, *44*
Truancy,
  drug abuse and, *59*
  legal definition of, *207, 338*
  repeat offenders, *288*
  sentencing options for, *64, 210, 212*
  seriousness of, *341*

U

Unemployment, *219*

V

Victims,
  See Restitution,

W

Weapons,
  deaths of juveniles from firearms, *300*
  misconduct with, *138, 323*
  possession of,
    arrests of juveniles for, *334*
    by female juveniles, *132, 151*

sentencing
  options for, *325*
in schools, *18, 151*
used in assaults, *275*

Z
Zero tolerance, *203*

www.ingramcontent.com/pod-product-compliance
Lightning Source LLC
Chambersburg PA
CBHW011747220426
43667CB00020B/2925